THE UNIVERSITY
OF CALIFORNIA PRESS

A CENTENNIAL BOOK

One hundred books
published between 1990 and 1995
bear this special imprint of
the University of California Press.
We have chosen each Centennial Book
as an example of the Press's finest
publishing and bookmaking traditions
as we celebrate the beginning of
our second century.

UNIVERSITY OF CALIFORNIA PRESS

Founded in 1893

The University of California in 1893, the year the Press began:
North Hall, Mechanic Arts Building, Bacon Art and Library
Building, South Hall. Only the last still exists today. Courtesy
University Archives, The Bancroft Library.

THE UNIVERSITY OF CALIFORNIA PRESS

The Early Years, 1893–1953

ALBERT MUTO

University of California Press

BERKELEY · LOS ANGELES · OXFORD

University of California Press
Berkeley and Los Angeles, California

University of California Press, Ltd.
Oxford, England

© 1993 by
The Regents of the University of California

CIP data appear at the end of the book

Printed in the United States of America

9 8 7 6 5 4 3 2 1

The paper used in this publication meets
the minimum requirements of American National
Standard for Information Sciences—Permanence of Paper
for Printed Library Materials, ANSI Z39.48-1984. ∞

For my sons,

Francesco, Antonio, Alessandro,

and

in memory of the first authors,

Andrew C. Lawson and Milicent Shinn,

who kept the fledgling press alive

in the nineteenth century

Contents

·   *Preface*   ·

This history follows the University of California Press
from its small beginnings in the nineteenth century to its
emergence in the mid 1950s as a modern scholarly publishing house. In these sixty years the Press underwent a
number of changes—some of them changes of character
drastic enough, perhaps, to justify the term used by one
director: metamorphoses.

The Press began as a sort of service agency, operated by
a faculty committee and issuing research papers for distribution by library exchange and gift. It then, after the reorganization of Manager Samuel T. Farquhar, became at-
tached to and dominated by a much larger printing plant;
together they produced a number of books notable for ex-
cellence of design and printing, while the research papers,
or monographs, remained the chief raison d'être. And finally, about 1953, and after an intra-university battle that
raged for several years, the Press, under the direction of
August Frugé, gained its independence from the printing
plant and emerged as a scholarly publishing house in the
Oxford-Cambridge tradition. That the above is an over-
simplified statement of a complex series of events will be
clear to the reader of the following pages.

Chapters 3 to 5 of this history are based on my dissertation for the School of Library and Information Studies,
Berkeley, completed in 1976.[1] That account is now much
shortened and greatly revised. Since the longer version
with full documentation may be consulted in the University of California Library at Berkeley, I have provided only
light annotation here, mostly of matters not specified in the
dissertation. The Introduction, on the rise of university
presses in America, is quite new, and much has been added
to the discussion of the first authors.

The chief primary sources are the Regents' Files and the
Correspondence and Papers of the Presidents, both in the
University Archives in the Bancroft Library; the Minutes
of the Academic Council, of the Academic Senate, and especially of the Editorial Committee of the Academic Senate, all in the Bancroft; the several versions of the *Rules of
the Editorial Committee*, in the same place; miscellaneous
historical papers preserved in the University Press files;
and the catalogs of Press publications; also, the collection
of Gilman Papers in the California Archives and in Special
Collections, Milton S. Eisenhower Library, the Johns
Hopkins University.

The history of the Press under Farquhar and during
Frugé's reorganization in the early 1950s was written several years later, mostly between 1988 and 1990, at the invitation of the Press. For obvious reasons it is more heavily

---

1. "The University of California Press, 1893–1933" (University of California, Berkeley, 1976).

annotated where sources are not clear from the text itself. I have taken particular care to substantiate my account of the more crucial events, based primarily on a detailed study of the papers of President Robert Gordon Sproul. Other written sources are the Minutes of the Editorial Committee from 1932 on; surviving historical papers at the Press; and the published and unpublished writings of August Frugé, who came to the Press in 1944 and headed it after 1949. Some of Frugé's papers, which I have used and referred to in their unpublished form, have been revised for inclusion in a volume of memoirs.

I have interviewed a number of people, such as the brother and the first wife of Samuel Farquhar, and Hazel Niehaus, who worked at the Press for nearly half a century and who provided me with clues that led to the finding of long-abandoned documents. I have also had the great advantage of several long interviews with Frugé, the chief surviving participant in the events after 1944. The facts in his recollections I have studiously checked against the documents he wrote at the time as well as against those of others in the presidents' papers; there are a few discrepancies—the inexactnesses of memory, it appears.

I am deeply grateful to August Frugé for his encouragement and cooperation. Also I would like to thank Robert D. Harlan and Fredric J. Mosher, professors of the history of printing and publishing at the School of Library and Information Studies, Berkeley, for their interest through the years. I am in debt to Lincoln Constance, professor emeritus of botany and long-time member of the Editorial Committee, for his analysis of the Scientific Series (Appendix 1), a debt acknowledged at several points in the pages that follow.

The writing would not have been possible without the help of the staff of the Bancroft Library, who provided me with the greater part of the documentation, particularly William M. Roberts, University archivist. At Johns Hopkins University my gratitude goes to Cynthia Requardt and Joan Grattan for their assistance.

CHAPTER 1

INTRODUCTION

The New American University and Its Press

THE FIRST AMERICAN UNIVERSITY PRESSES were not fashioned after Oxford and Cambridge, venerable as the latter were. Publishing needs were then simpler. At the "new" American universities, formed or re-formed in the late nineteenth century to emphasize advanced study, the dissemination of new knowledge became an essential function, as it was in German and other continental schools. Faculty members were often required to publish, and graduate students encouraged to do so. Since there were few publishers in this country who welcomed specialized writings, it was soon seen to be the reponsibility of the parent universities to publish—or at least to print—what these scholars produced.

The nineteenth-century beginning of scholarly publishing, although hesitant and informal, was real, and a number of large modern presses trace their origins to this time. Later, in the early twentieth century, other new presses were established—a second wave, so to speak—as book-publishing organizations more or less in the Oxbridge mold.

It is generally agreed that the first American university to make publishing a regular activity was Johns Hopkins in 1878. More than a decade after Hopkins and at about the same time in the early 1890s, Chicago, Columbia, and California all made a beginning. Hopkins and Chicago started with journals; the first publication at Columbia was a festschrift; California issued monographs in series. All four eventually became book publishers of consequence, but we shall see that California's monograph press, perhaps because limited to local scholars, proved the most difficult to convert to a modern form. The early journals of Hopkins and Chicago were broadly conceived and still flourish.

Before the mentioned dates a few universities or colleges set up small printing plants, manned mostly by students in connection with the study of journalism. Some of them printed university internal publications. Cornell established a short-lived plant in 1869, even printing a few books before dissolution in 1884. The California plant, opened in 1874, may have been modeled on the one at Cornell, since the two presidents, Daniel Coit Gilman and Andrew D. White, were in close communication. But none of these plants bore any parental relationship to the later publication of scholarship and need not be called forerunners. Also, some branches of universities, such as the Lick Observatory in California, issued reports that did not lead to anything else. Although it is not always possible to identify the true moment of genesis, especially when early intentions and later reality are vastly different, we may assume

Student printers in North Hall, 1874. Courtesy University
Archives, The Bancroft Library.

here that only the regular publication of scholarly papers
or books constituted the genuine beginning of a press.

It was the rise of the American university in the nineteenth
century that made the university press inevitable. Our colleges, by whatever name, existed primarily for the education of young men, a valuable and important task but quite
different from the goals of the universities that succeeded
them. The change from one to the other is not much more
than a hundred years old.

Without seeking to analyze the causes or to trace the steps of the transformation, we may note some of the factors that lay behind it or accompanied it. First, there was the great worldwide, or at least Europe-wide, growth of interest in science, including experimental science and observation of the natural and physical world. Beginning perhaps in the seventeenth century and continuing through the Enlightenment of the eighteenth, scientific study grew immensely in the nineteenth century. Thus, to cite only one example, the publication of Darwin's *On the Origin of Species* in 1859 was the culmination of a long interest in evolution and the mechanisms that made it work.

In England scientists and scholars tended to be private individuals of means, but on the continent, and especially in Germany, advanced study became centered in the great universities, which developed into research institutions of a kind that existed nowhere else. Many serious American students went to Germany for graduate study, and it was natural that they should return with ideas about making over the schools of their own country.

In the latter part of the century, and for one reason or another, American men of great wealth took to endowing new universities. Thus, among others, Cornell University in 1865, Vanderbilt in 1872, Johns Hopkins in 1875, and Stanford in 1891 were founded by men of those names, and the University of Chicago in 1892 by John D. Rockefeller.[1]

1. The dates found in university histories and reference works vary slightly, some being the years of chartering, others the years of first teaching.

All became great institutions, worthy rivals of the old private schools of the east and the newer state universities. Some of them, including Cornell and California, benefited from the Morrill Act of 1862, which granted federal land for the establishment of colleges that would offer programs in agriculture and other technical subjects as well as in the traditional academic fields.

It is worth mentioning that women were being accepted in some universities. In October 1870 the Regents of the University of California voted unanimously to admit women "on equal terms in all respects."

Working to bring about the change in higher education were many noted scholars and administrators, including, among others, Andrew D. White at Cornell, William Rainey Harper at Chicago, Charles W. Eliot at Harvard, and James B. Angell at Michigan. A little later came David Starr Jordan at Stanford and Benjamin Ide Wheeler at California, both recruited from Cornell.

But in many ways the central figure and perhaps the most influential of all was Daniel Coit Gilman, a man of vision and ability who had the good fortune to be given free rein by the trustees of a new university, quite free of either legislative or traditional restrictions. Under him Johns Hopkins became something like the model and ideal of the new university. In tribute to Gilman on the university's twenty-fifth anniversary, Woodrow Wilson, a former Hopkins student and the president of Princeton University, delivered a congratulatory address in the name of the alumni and faculty. He said, "You were the first to create and organize in America a university in which the discovery and dissemination of new truths were conceded a rank superior to mere instruction, and in which the efficiency and value of research as an educational instrument were exemplified in the training of many investigators."

On the same occasion Charles W. Eliot said, "I want to testify that the graduate school of Harvard University, started feebly in 1870 and 1871, did not thrive until the example of Johns Hopkins forced our Faculty to put their strength into the development of our instruction for graduates. And what was true of Harvard was true of every other university in the land which aspired to create an advanced school of arts and sciences."[2]

Gilman was a graduate of Yale College who spent some time observing European universities and then returned to New Haven, where he was for a time librarian at Yale and professor at the Sheffield Scientific School. He became secretary of the latter, worked to raise funds, and participated in the rapid development of the school. Recalling that experience, he later wrote of "the changes which were introduced at Yale in the fifties and sixties, the grafting of a new branch . . . upon the old stock."[3] Then in 1872 he became the second president of the new University of California,

2. The quotations are in *Johns Hopkins University: Celebration of the Twenty-Fifth Anniversary of the Founding of the University* (Baltimore, 1902), 39 and 105.
3. Daniel Coit Gilman, *The Launching of a University* (New York, 1906), 4.

where he stayed for two and a half years, surviving a serious political controversy in his second year. Short as was his stay, he left an impression in Berkeley that persisted for many years and had much to do with later developments there and with the beginning of the University of California Press.

Because of the turbulent political climate in California in the 1870s, Gilman resigned and accepted the presidency of Johns Hopkins. "Baltimore afforded an opportunity to develop a private endowment free from ecclesiastical or political control, where from the beginning the old and the new, the humanities and the sciences, theory and practice, could be generously promoted."[4]

In an interview with the Hopkins trustees at the end of 1874, about a month before Gilman accepted their invitation to become first president of the new university, he proposed the establishment of a graduate school staffed by research scholars who would be expected to publish. An article in the *Nation* of 28 January 1875 reported the substance of that interview:

> He would make it the means of promoting scholarship of the first order, and this by only offering the kind of instruction to advanced students which other universities offer in their post-graduate courses. . . . For this purpose he would select as professors men now standing in the front rank of their own fields . . . and he would exact from them yearly proof of the diligent and fruitful cultivation of their specialties by

4. Ibid.

compelling them to print somewhere the results of their researches.[5]

As these ideas were refined and modified, it proved desirable from the outset to offer undergraduate as well as graduate instruction. The emphasis, however, remained on the
latter and on research leading to publication in the tradition
of the German universities. In fall 1876 the first teaching
staff of twenty-eight met with the first student body of
fifty-four graduate and thirty-five undergraduate students.

Nine months earlier, in January 1876, Gilman wrote in
his First Annual Report to the trustees: "The idea is not
lost sight of that the power of the University will depend
upon the character of its resident staff of permanent professors. It is their researches in the library and the laboratory . . . their publications through the journals and the
scientific treatises which will make the University in Baltimore an attraction to the best students, and serviceable to
the intellectual growth of the land."

Publishing began two years later with the first number
of *American Journal of Mathematics*. Shortly thereafter came
the *American Chemical Journal*, the *American Journal of
Philology*, and the *Journal of Modern Languages*. Historical
monographs were issued in a series called Studies in His-

---

5. Quoted in Fabian Franklin, *The Life of Daniel Coit Gilman* (New York,
1910), 188–89. Present-day writers who argue that the pendulum has
swung too far from teaching may note that Gilman was no uncritical
advocate of research. "It may be," he said, "the highest occupation of
the human mind. It may be the most insignificant." (*Johns Hopkins University*, 24.)

tory and Politics. Other works were issued separately. From the beginning it was decided that the journals would be open to contributions from any part of the country, a generous provision that ensured their continuing importance as national and not local publications.[6]

"The university without a printing press would be like an orator without a voice," said Gilman in an address printed in the *Evening Bulletin* of 23 February 1878. And he went on to explain that it was no longer necessary to maintain a printing plant: printing could be purchased; the need was to publish. Only through its published research could the university achieve one of its highest goals, the dissemination of knowledge beyond its own walls.

Wide distribution was achieved by exchange with other universities, particularly with foreign ones since most American universities had little to offer in return. Other partners were learned societies and scientific academies. Under the conditions of one hundred years ago, it is clear that exchange, rather than sale, was the most effective way, perhaps the only feasible way, of distributing specialized scholarly publications.

6. Gilman, *The Launching of a University*, 115–17.

CHAPTER 2

PUBLISHING BEGINS
IN BERKELEY

Chartered in 1868, three years after the Civil War,
the University of California held its first classes in Oakland
in the following year, with ten faculty members and forty
students. The first faculty member hired by the regents
was John LeConte, a former officer in the Confederate
Army. The first man elected president was George B.
McClellan, a Union general.

When the general declined to serve, the regents elected
Daniel Coit Gilman, then of the Sheffield Scientific School
at Yale. He, too, declined, but two years later, on the resignation of the first president, Henry Durant, Gilman accepted a second offer and came to Oakland. There and on
the new campus in Berkeley he served as president for
nearly three years.

Controversy arrived in his second year. The farmers of
the state, represented in the legislature by a political party
known as the Grangers, wished to turn the University into
a technical school, while Gilman fought to organize it in a
more comprehensive and liberal way. Some newspapers
wrote of "President Gilman and the kid-glove junta" and
charged him with "teaching rich lawyers' boys Greek with

the farmers' money."[1] Two members of the faculty joined in the attack. There was a legislative enquiry into the management of the University and its funds.

Although the regents and most of the faculty stood firm and the attack was repelled, it had an effect on Gilman. In a letter of resignation in 1874 he wrote, "For University fighting I have had no training; in University work I delight." And to his friend Andrew D. White of Cornell, "We came out all right last winter, but the perils of a college subject to direct legislative control are so great, so complex, so inevitable, that I am in no mood to go forward here."[2] Gilman was dissuaded from his first resignation, but in the following year he went to Johns Hopkins with a free hand to develop the kind of new university he believed in.

In 1879 the University of California was given a new standing in the state constitution, freeing it from the direct political control of the legislature. And in 1887 a permanent tax was established for its support.

Gilman retained a loyal following in California. In 1891, sixteen years after he went to Baltimore, Regent George J. Ainsworth asked him to return to Berkeley as president, writing, "You have the entire confidence of every member of the Board of Regents. You can have your own way in everything."[3] And in the following year Milicent W.

1. Milicent W. Shinn, "The University of California," *The Overland Monthly* (October–December 1892): 357.
2. The quotations are from Franklin, *The Life of Daniel Coit Gilman*, 161 and 163.
3. Ainsworth to Gilman, 13 June 1891, in Gilman Papers, Bancroft Library (Archives).

Daniel Coit Gilman. San Francisco, 1875. Courtesy
University Archives, The Bancroft Library.

Joseph C. Rowell. 1874. Courtesy University
Archives, The Bancroft Library.

Shinn, a freshman during the president's last year, wrote in the *Overland Monthly*, "The regret when he went away was sharp and bitter; in the long struggle that followed, he was always looked back to as the lost leader. . . . The period of his administration became the golden age of University tradition to a degree that made a real embarrassment to successors."[4]

When Joseph C. Rowell graduated in 1874 he became lecturer in English history, recorder to the faculty, and secretary to President Gilman. In the following year Rowell became the University's first full-time librarian, and from that post he kept in touch with Gilman, followed his progress, and asked for Hopkins publications. In his report to the president in 1886 Rowell made what may have been the first clear call for publishing at California: "The need of establishing some kind of University bulletin or other publication wherein can be published results of research and work by members of the various faculties, and even certain kinds of work by students, as a medium of exchange is respectfully alluded to."

Meanwhile, Hopkins graduates joined the faculty in Berkeley and helped to carry Gilman's idea of a university to the west coast. Josiah Royce, an 1875 graduate of California, followed Gilman to Hopkins in 1876 as one of the first fellows, and two years later, along with three others, received the degree of Ph.D., the first conferred by that university. Returning to Berkeley as an instructor in En-

4. Shinn, "The University of California," 358.

glish literature, he remained four years before going to Harvard and to eventual fame as a writer and teacher of philosophy. Royce seems to have had considerable influence on President William T. Reid (1881–85), who in his first annual report to the governor stressed the need for faculty members who could do original work.

After Royce came others from Hopkins. Charles H. Levermore came in 1886 as an instructor in political economy and stayed two years. Irving Stringham, professor of mathematics, arrived in 1882 and remained until his death in 1909. In 1887, along with President Edward Singleton Holden and Professor Martin Kellogg, he proposed a college of pure science, an idea that bore fruit some years later. Most important of all, perhaps, was Andrew C. Lawson, who became a key figure in the reorganization of undergraduate science instruction, the establishment of graduate courses in geology, and the beginning of the University of California Press. He became the first author of the Press.

Born in Scotland and schooled in Canada, Lawson graduated from the University of Toronto in 1883, joined the Canadian Geological Survey, and somehow found time to publish a number of papers and to complete doctoral work at Johns Hopkins in 1888. In 1890, while working in Vancouver, he wrote to Joseph LeConte, professor of geology and perhaps the most notable member of the Berkeley faculty, asking whether there might be an opening at the University. Among the testimonials he enclosed was one from W. C. Brögger of Stockholm, who wrote, "Dr. Lawson

Andrew Lawson on the Mother Lode. 1903. Francis E.
Vaughan, *Andrew C. Lawson: Scientist, Teacher, Philosopher*
(Glendale, Calif.: Arthur H. Clark, 1970).

belongs to those who discover the new." LeConte was impressed, and before the year was out Lawson was appointed assistant professor of mineralogy and geology. LeConte has been quoted as saying that he brought the young man to California to develop the scientific side of the subject so that he could devote himself to the philosophic side.[5]

With tremendous energy Lawson threw himself into the organization of courses, soon proposing one in field geology, perhaps the first of its kind in this country. And at the end of his first year he introduced the department's first graduate course, described by the Academic Council in part as "prosecution of original research and publication of results." That latter requirement, quite unusual then or now, was central to Lawson's thinking. Action soon followed words. In the summer of 1892 Lawson went with a student, Juan de la Cruz Posada, to study the region around Monterey, returning with the manuscript that was to become the first bulletin of the Department of Geology and the first publication of the University of California Press. Other geological monographs were ready about the same time.

Lacking specific documentation, one cannot know who talked to whom or what motivated the regents of the University to make the first appropriation for publishing, but given Lawson's activities, his determination and great en-

5. Lawson to LeConte, 4 September 1890, in Regents' Files, Bancroft Library (Archives). National Academy of Sciences, *Biographical Memoirs* 37: 186–87.

Lawson's first field trip. Carmel, spring 1892. Standing second
from the left is Juan de la Cruz Posada of Medellín, Colombia,
joint author, with Lawson, of the first publication of the Press.
Two of the women in the party are students; the third, kneeling at
the right, is Mrs. Lawson. Photograph by Andrew Lawson.
Francis E. Vaughan, *Andrew C. Lawson: Scientist, Teacher,
Philosopher* (Glendale, Calif.: Arthur H. Clark, 1970).

ergy, it seems likely that he was the prime mover, or at least
one of those whose demands led to the establishment of the
publishing program that became a press.

The formal beginning took place in February 1893,
when the Board of Regents made an appropriation for the
publication of research monographs written by the faculty.
Two days later J. Harmon Bonté, secretary of the board,
wrote to President Martin Kellogg:

> The following is a copy from the report of the Committee on
> Internal Administration submitted at the meeting of the
> Board of Regents held the 14th instant:
>   "Your Committee, believing that it is often desirable to

publish papers prepared by members of the Faculty, begs leave to submit the following recommendations:

1. The sum of $1,000 shall be appropriated in the annual Budget for the printing of monographs, etc. prepared by members of the Faculty of the University.

2. There shall be a Committee of five members of the Faculty, to be appointed by the President who himself shall be a member and ex-officio chairman of such Committee, whose duty it shall be to pass upon all papers submitted for publication, and to determine all questions arising with reference to the same." Approved.

When Kellogg read the letter at a meeting of the Academic Council he pointed out that the money would become available on 1 July and said that members of the faculty could submit manuscripts to the Committee on Publications, which he would appoint at once. Professor Lawson then asked whether works by graduate students might also be published. The council so recommended and the regents approved.[6]

A month before this general action by the regents, the board had voted to advance the sum of $200 to pay for printing a pamphlet by Isaac Flagg, associate professor of Greek. Although this advance was a separate action and was supposed to be repaid from sales receipts, the amount was included as part of the $1,000 appropriation in the budget for 1893–94. Flagg had the printing done in Boston, and the booklet, entitled *Outlines of the Temporal and*

6. In the academic year 1893–94 there were 164 faculty members and 815 students, of whom 64 were graduates.

President Martin Kellogg (above) and the other two members of
the first Committee on Publications, George Holmes Howison and
Washington Irving Stringham (opposite). Courtesy University
Archives, The Bancroft Library.

George Holmes Howison   Washington Irving Stringham

Modal Principles of Attic Prose, was placed on sale there and at the student store in Berkeley in June or July 1893. Although it bore the imprint "Published by the University," the Committee on Publications seems to have had nothing to do with it, nor did it ever appear in any Press catalog, not even the "complete" catalog of 1893–1943. A classroom aid rather than a research monograph, it may be considered an isolated publication and not one of the first scholarly works. It came out a month or two after the first two geology bulletins.

The scholarly publications of that first year, 1893, were four bulletins of the Department of Geology and a monograph on child development by Milicent W. Shinn, a graduate student. Number 1 of the bulletins, dated May 1893, was *The Geology of Carmelo Bay*, by Lawson, with contributions by the student Posada. Number 2, with the same date, was a short paper by another student, Charles Palache. Two others, one by Lawson, came out in December. In the first two years, there were ten bulletins, three by Lawson, one by Joseph LeConte, and the rest by graduate students.

That first appropriation could hardly suffice for Lawson's ambitions, even if he had used all of it, and there was no other publication fund until regular grants started in 1901. But Lawson was not easily stopped. As early as September 1893 he asked President Kellogg for permission to take subscriptions for the first volume of the bulletin, the proceeds to be used for printing the second volume. Permission denied, he asked the regents to divert funds intended for preparation of a relief map. And in February of the following year he wrote to Regent Arthur Rodgers, expressing the need for an annual fund of at least $1,000 for geological research and publication.[7]

If all these sums appear small to us, and the work accomplished with them large, we should remember that the dollar of the 1890s was worth many times that of the 1990s. The first two geology papers, seventy pages in length, were composed and printed for $208.10. Lawson's sold for twenty-five cents and that by Palache for ten cents.

However he got the money, Lawson managed to keep the bulletin going until the turn of the century and the availability of regular funds. We might say, in retrospect, that he managed—with some help from Milicent Shinn— to keep the University Press going. And a hundred years later, as another century runs to an end, the Bulletin of the Department of Geology, now called Publications in Geological Sciences, is still alive, with more than 130 volumes cataloged.

A second monograph series began in 1893. Called University of California Studies and later renamed Publications in Education, its first number was *Notes on the Development of a Child* by Milicent Washburn Shinn, a most remarkable graduate student. Nearly twenty years earlier, as we have seen, Shinn was a freshman during Daniel Coit Gilman's last year in Berkeley. She interrupted her studies to teach in a country school for a while. She graduated in

7. Lawson, Correspondence and Papers, Bancroft Library.

Lawson, first author of the Press, at age 89.
Photograph by G. Paul Bishop, 1950. Francis
E. Vaughan, *Andrew C. Lawson: Scientist,
Teacher, Philosopher* (Glendale, Calif.: Arthur H.
Clark, 1970).

1880 and three years later became editor of the *Overland
Monthly*, a magazine of general interest that prided itself on
being representative of the whole west coast. She held that
post until 1894, several years after her return to the University as a graduate student.

While at the *Overland*, Shinn wrote two pieces that

showed her great devotion to the University, one an editorial promoting, among other things, donations for a women's gymnasium, a school of education, and research. The other, published in 1892, was a three-part history of the University, perhaps the first serious work of its kind, wherein she pointed out the need for a building plan, several years before the competition suggested by Bernard Maybeck and financed by Phoebe Apperson Hearst.[8]

In 1890 Shinn took two important steps: she returned to the University to pursue graduate studies, and she started a long research project that resulted in a number of publications and also led to her doctor's degree, the first granted by the University to a woman. "The work began," she wrote later, "with the birth of a girl babe in the house in which I lived. Within a half hour I began taking notes relating to her development, and these notes were continued daily throughout the first three years of her life."[9] Shinn lived in Niles, a small town near Oakland and now part of Fremont. The baby was her niece, Ruth.

At that time the graduate curriculum was small and in Shinn's field nonexistent. In June 1890 she wrote to President Gilman in Baltimore that she was working up with Professor Bernard Moses a graduate seminar that might,

8. The first piece was "Some Points for Californians Contemplating Endowments" in the November 1891 issue. The second, "The University of California," was published in the October–December 1892 issues.
9. Quoted in Grant T. Skelley, *"The Overland Monthly* Under Milicent Washburn Shinn, 1883–1894" (Ph.D. dissertation, University of California, Berkeley, 1968), 35.

Milicent W. Shinn. Graduation portrait, ca.
1880. Courtesy University Archives, The
Bancroft Library.

she thought, become the nucleus of a graduate department.
And there was established two years later the Department
of Pedagogy, with a single professor, Elmer Ellsworth
Brown. Milicent Shinn threw herself into the work of the
department as both student and organizer. Writing to
Phoebe Apperson Hearst, who shared an interest in child
education, she tried to promote new appointments and encouraged, without success, the endowment of a school of
education and a building to house it.[10]

10. Shinn to Gilman, 5 June 1890, in Gilman Papers, Johns Hopkins
University; Shinn to Hearst, 14 March 1893 and 14 January 1896, in
Hearst, Correspondence and Papers, Bancroft Library.

Mrs. Hearst, long dedicated to the cause of education, established and maintained kindergarten schools in San Francisco, Washington, D.C., and Lead, South Dakota, where her principal mining interests were located. In the capital, where she lived when her husband was a senator from California, she endowed a training class for kindergarten teachers and gave money for the building of the National Cathedral School. After the death of Senator Hearst in 1891, she returned to California, settling in Pleasanton, not far from Berkeley. Her interest in the University of California was particularly marked. For almost thirty years she lent a ready sympathy to the needs of the young institution. Appointed the first woman regent in 1897, she served on the board until her death in 1919.

Among her many gifts to the University, she sponsored a competition for the development of a plan for the Berkeley campus and erected the Hearst Mining Building in honor of her husband. Victor Henderson, secretary of the regents, recorded that she had, by 1914, spent twice as much for permanent buildings for the University as had the state itself. Underlying her great generosity was a deep personal interest in the students, particularly the women, whom she provided with scholarships, recreational facilities, and a gymnasium known as Hearst Hall.[11] Not least among the women befriended by Mrs. Hearst was Milicent Shinn.

11. "University Record" in the *University of California Chronicle*, 1914, p. 314, and 1919, pp. 58–59.

When the publishing appropriation was made in early 1893, Shinn was ready with the first part of her *Notes on the Development of a Child*. It came out in the fall of that year, with a second part in 1894. Both were eminently successful and were reprinted a number of times. There were more parts to come, and Shinn, like Andrew Lawson, was soon faced with the lack of funds to continue publishing. She made the situation known to Mrs. Hearst, perhaps hoping for influence on the regents, but help came in the form of a personal gift. With some embarrassment, Shinn accepted, more for the University than for herself, she said, and asked permission to call the new work a "joint publication, you supplying the money and I the work."[12]

Mrs. Hearst gave $300, from which Shinn not only managed to publish her parts 3 and 4, issued together in 1899, but before that, in 1897, to bring out *Notes on Children's Drawings*, edited by Elmer E. Brown and written by Shinn and three other members of the graduate seminar in pedagogy. This was made volume 2, number 1, of the monograph series. Mrs. Hearst agreed that sales receipts could be used for further publishing.

In December 1898, the year before the publication of Shinn's *Notes*, parts 3 and 4, she received her doctorate magna cum laude, with the major subject of her oral being "child study in its bearing on pedagogy." It was, Shinn

12. Shinn to Hearst, 14 January 1896, in Hearst, Correspondence and Papers, Bancroft Library.

Milicent Shinn with her niece Ruth W. Shinn, the principal
subject of her studies. Ca. 1897. Lyla M. Hunt, *Shinn
Historical Park: Souvenir History*, 1976. Courtesy Robert B.
Fisher, M.D.

supposed, the only Ph.D. on this subject in the world. Recalling the experience in 1925, she said, "No one was qual-
ified to teach me: there were no predecessors in the study
of a baby's mind. But we studied together, two or three
professors and I . . . and finally we had all decided that I
had done enough work to qualify as a full fledged doctor of
philosophy. . . . I don't think that ever before or since a
woman has taken the degree when the professors have had
to study with her, using her own books and notes as texts,
in order to grant the degree. We often laughed about the
situation."[13]

After receiving the degree Shinn wrote a twelve-part series of articles in *Puritan* magazine entitled *The Biography of
a Baby* and published as a book by Houghton Mifflin in
1900. This attracted the attention of Herbert Spencer, who
requested further data for the revision of his *Psychology*. She
also worked on revising her dissertation, a continuation of
Notes, finished it in 1903, but was not able to publish until
five years later.

At first Shinn tried to publish the book herself, sending
the manuscript to Pacific Press Publishing Company in
Oakland, where 115 pages had been set up by the spring
of 1906. "The earthquake threw it all down," she wrote to
Joseph Rowell, "broke my electro plates and pied all that
was not electroed." After some delay the printers went at
it again and had the entire work set up, proofed and re-

13. *Oakland Examiner*, 26 January 1925.

proofed, when their plant caught fire and burned to the ground. Shinn then asked Rowell whether the University could publish her book. "I've no doubt," she wrote, "that to undertake it will bring down earthquake and fire on any printing office, but it has to be risked."[14]

But by now Shinn had no standing at the University, and the Editorial Committee, which had succeeded the Committee on Publications, questioned her eligibility. F. B. Dresslar, one of her former professors, gave her work the department's blessing, and Rowell attested to her right to use sales receipts from the publications financed by Mrs. Hearst. Printed at last in Pennsylvania, Shinn's *Notes on the Development of a Child II* came out in 1908 as volume 4 of Publications in Education.

Milicent Shinn and Andrew Lawson, graduate student and professor, did much to develop the University as a center of graduate study in their fields. And it was their efforts, more than those of any others, that kept the University's publishing program going through the last years of the nineteenth century, relying for nearly a decade on the single appropriation of $1,000.

In 1916 the first manager of the press, Albert Allen, wrote in his annual report, "The University of California was among the first to recognize the obligation to promote scholarship by fostering with its own means, opportunities of publication. . . . This plan of publishing contributions

14. Shinn to Rowell, 18 August 1906, in University Press files.

from members of the University community in departmental series . . . , if it did not originate here, has been
more highly developed at California than at any other institution known to the writer."[15] That development came
in the twenty-year regime of President Benjamin Ide
Wheeler.

15. Minutes of the Editorial Committee of the Academic Senate, 445.
Hereinafter cited as Minutes.

Phoebe Apperson Hearst and President Benjamin Ide
Wheeler on commencement day, 1913. Courtesy University
Archives, The Bancroft Library.

CHAPTER 3

THE MONOGRAPH PRESS OF
BENJAMIN IDE WHEELER

W HEELER WAS A NEW ENGLANDER who took his first two degrees at Brown University and then spent four years studying classical philology at Berlin, Leipzig, Jena, and at Heidelberg, where he received the Ph.D. degree summa cum laude. He thereupon taught German for a year at Harvard and then spent thirteen years at Cornell as professor of Greek and comparative philology. When in 1899 he was offered the presidency of the University of California, he accepted only after the regents agreed to conditions that clearly defined the functions of the regents and the president, giving the president what amounted to dictatorial powers. He was to be the only point of communication between the faculty and the regents; he alone was to have power to select and dismiss professors and other teachers; he demanded the support of the regents in all matters pertaining to the faculty, regardless of any differences of opinion that might arise at meetings of the board; and finally he was to be in charge of all nonacademic employees, from the highest administrators to the lowest clerks. Wheeler vigorously exercised these powers throughout his presidency, an absolute ruler until the end.

Wheeler's administration was wittily summarized many years later by Arthur E. Hutson, professor of English and secretary of the Academic Senate:

> He hired, promoted, and dismissed as he chose, without consulting the faculty; he appointed the committees of the senate; he dominated educational policy, again without consultation of some of the best scholarly minds in the world; he presided over meetings of the council and the senate, at which he was likely to grant the privilege of the floor only to those who agreed with him. He is said, also, to have reprimanded a professor who appeared on campus without a hat.[1]

When Wheeler was invited to California he must have known something of how earlier presidents had fared. After the departure of Daniel Coit Gilman in 1875 there ensued for the next eighteen years a period that the historian Verne Stadtman has called the Era of Powerless Presidents, during which five presidents and acting presidents were appointed by the regents, who exercised the power themselves through committees, while quarreling among themselves. The most powerful officer, more than any of the presidents, was the secretary of the regents.[2] That the need for a stronger presidency was recognized by some at least is shown by Regent Ainsworth's letter to Gilman in 1891, mentioned in Chapter 2, which asked him to return and promised that he could have his own way in everything.

1. *The Centennial Record of the University of California* (Berkeley, 1967), 290.
2. Verne A. Stadtman, *The University of California, 1868–1968* (New York, 1970), 88–106.

President Wheeler rides his horse on campus. Courtesy
University Archives, The Bancroft Library.

Partial reform came about under Martin Kellogg, who served as acting president for three years and then as president from 1893 to 1899. Kellogg, a long-time professor of Greek, got along well with the faculty, ran a competent and low-key administration, and managed to serve until he was seventy, longer than any of his predecessors. Under him the president's powers were somewhat increased. They were made virtually complete under his successor, Benjamin Ide Wheeler, a man of great prestige, who had been offered other important posts. Wheeler seems to have been a natural autocrat, whose nature was reinforced by German training.

In spite of—perhaps in part because of—his manner of working, Wheeler accomplished much for the University. During his twenty years student enrollment and faculty membership both trebled; the faculty increasing from 177 to 693. Eleven new granite or concrete buildings went up on the campus, five of them, including the large Doe Library, financed by private gift. The University Farm in Davis, the Citrus Experiment Station in Riverside, and the Scripps Institution at La Jolla were established. A graduate division, an extension division, and twenty new departments were organized. Research funds were made available to the faculty.

Wheeler not only sought out excellent scholars but also saw to it that the regents provided funds to publish the results of their research. The second publishing grant—after the original $1,000 in 1893—was $3,000 for the fiscal year 1901–2. There followed annual appropriations to what was

known officially as the Publications Fund but was referred
to as, among other things, the Series Fund. At some later
time it became known colloquially and then officially as
the Scientific Account. By whatever name, the fund grew.
By the end of the first decade of the new century, it
amounted to almost $10,000, and during the second de-
cade, it tripled to $30,000. None of these amounts in-
clude the special funds for the Semicentennial Publications
or the publishing funds given by private individuals, such
as Mrs. Hearst.

Generously tended at last, monographs sprang up like
spring flowers in a good season. In addition to the two old
series in geology and education, three new series began in
1902, three more in 1903, two in 1904, and one or more in
every succeeding year through 1913. By the end of that
year publications were appearing in twenty-three subject
series.[3] And among the new ones were many of those destined, along with Geology, to become the most voluminous
and prestigious publications of the old Press: Botany and
Zoology in 1902, Entomology in 1906, the great trio of
series in the life sciences; American Archaeology and
Ethnology in 1903; Classical Philology—Wheeler's own
field—in 1904. Semitic Philology came in 1907 and Modern Philology in 1909, along with a number of others that

3. Not included in these figures are a number of publications listed in
catalogs and bearing the imprint of the Press, for which the Press acted
principally as producer and distributor but exercised little control.
Among them are the astronomical publications of the Lick Observatory,
the publications of the Academy of Pacific Coast History (Bancroft Library), and several series of lectures and prize essays.

proved useful in smaller measure. The word "philology," now gone out of fashion, must have been a favorite during Wheeler's time. But of the series using that designation, only one—the modern one—has survived to the present, the others having been merged into broader collections.

Several of the new series owed their existence to Phoebe Apperson Hearst, who had already helped finance papers in child development. She was a diligent collector of art and antiquities, all destined for presentation to the University, and in the years around the turn of the century she financed exploratory expeditions to old- and new-world sites. It was the great accumulation of returning material that brought about the founding of the anthropology museum. From the explorations in Egypt came a series of publications in Graeco-Roman archaeology and another in Egyptian archaeology, both paid for by Mrs. Hearst. Begun in 1902, the first was entirely devoted to publication of the Tebtunis Papyri, three volumes in four, while the second described the findings in the early dynastic cemeteries at Naga-ed-Dér. Its first volume appeared in 1905, and the last, the seventh, came as a surprise to Press officers in 1965. (Exploration had ended in 1906.) These two series of large quarto volumes, cloth-bound and printed in Germany and England, were in form quite unlike the other series and might have been called books rather than monographs had the president been anyone but Benjamin Ide Wheeler.

The combined museum and Department of Anthropology was set up in 1901, with all salaries and expenses paid by Mrs. Hearst until 1908. The first class, taught by the young Alfred L. Kroeber, destined to be the University's greatest name in anthropology, was held in 1902 in Berkeley, although the museum itself was in San Francisco. The new department's chief research interest, deemed appropriate for a state university, was the prehistory, languages, ethnic customs, and types of the native peoples of California and adjacent regions. And so, again with the financial support of Mrs. Hearst, there was begun in 1903 the monograph series entitled American Archaeology and Ethnology, a publication famous in the field and one that ran to fifty volumes and several hundred papers before it was superseded in 1964 by the more broadly named Publications in Anthropology.

The very first paper, by P. E. Goddard, was on the life, culture, and texts of the Hupa Indians of northwestern California. In the second volume were four papers by Kroeber; in fact, he dominated the first twenty volumes of the series. The twentieth itself, published in 1923, commemorated the twentieth anniversary of the organization of the department and the museum and was entitled *Phoebe Apperson Hearst Memorial Volume.*[4]

It is worth noting that the Indian Ishi, the last survivor of his tribe, became the ward of the department in 1912 and lived out the last years of his life in the museum in San Francisco, which had survived the earthquake and fire of

---

4. Some of the information above comes from the "Historical Introduction" to that volume.

1906. *Ishi in Two Worlds* (1961), the celebrated account by Theodora Kroeber and the first best-selling book of the Press, was based on several papers in the AAE series as well as on the recollections of her husband.

The series entitled Publications in Botany began in 1902 with *A Botanical Survey of San Jacinto Mountain* by H. M. Hall and was then dominated for several years by the pioneer studies of Pacific seaweeds by W. A. Setchell and N. L. Gardner. Other noted contributors in the early years were W. L. Jepson, known for the great flora, and T. H. Goodspeed, whose contributions to the cytology of tobacco (*Nicotiana*) continued from 1912 to 1954. Setchell served as sole editor of the series for the first two decades. The series is still alive, with about eighty volumes published, although it became much less active after recent changes in University research patterns.[5]

Publications in Zoology, which began in the same year, have slowed for the same reason. Many early contributions were on marine animals, corresponding to the exploration of marine algae in the botany series, and many of them came from San Diego, where the Scripps Institution became part of the University in 1912. Meanwhile in Berkeley there was established the Museum of Vertebrate Zoology, supported by another angel, Annie M. Alexander. The first director was Joseph Grinnell, another great early name in Berkeley science. From the museum came many

5. A more detailed account of the monograph series as a whole and of many individual series may be found in Appendix 1.

systematic and ecological studies, some of them deriving from expeditions to Alaska and elsewhere, sponsored by Miss Alexander. In addition to series monographs, Grinnell and his associates produced a number of books, including *The Game Birds of California*, issued in 1918 as one of the Semicentennial Publications, and *Animal Life in the Yosemite*, a separate volume that appeared in 1924, after Wheeler's retirement. In 1937 came *Fur-Bearing Mammals of California* (two volumes), by Grinnell and others. Although no longer very active, the Zoology series goes on, with more than one hundred volumes in print.

The third great monograph series in the life sciences, Entomology, began in 1906 with technical papers from the Agricultural Experiment Station on insects of economic importance. Later there came many large taxonomic studies by, among others, E. G. Linsley and R. L. Usinger. The latter, as chairman of the Editorial Committee at a critical time, played a large role in the later transformation of the Press (Chapter 11). The vast number and variety of insect species have led to numerous well-illustrated descriptive papers, the sort of publication best suited to a monograph series. This one continues, with more than a hundred volumes to its credit.

It was learned years later that monograph publication was not acceptable to writers in many humanistic fields, but in those early days scholars were beginning to produce short studies of ancient texts and other aspects of literature, language, and history, the kind of work done in Germany.

It is still done of course and appears in journals like those started at Chicago and Johns Hopkins. But in Berkeley in 1904 a series in classical philology was started, and in the following year Wheeler himself contributed the third number of the first volume, a brief paper entitled *The Whence and Whither of the Modern Science of Language*. The series went on for many years; later a companion series was started in classical archaeology, and in 1965 the two were combined into the Classical Studies series. Although publication in the classical field, which continues vigorously today, turned largely to books after Wheeler's departure, the series remains for studies that are too long for journals and not feasible as books.

The reader may wonder at the proliferation of a kind of university publication so different from the models in Oxford and Cambridge, from those of the new American university presses of the early twentieth century, or even from commercial book publication in America. But in Berkeley publishing was more than noncommercial; it might have been called anticommercial. Distribution was mostly by gift and exchange, to the great benefit of the University library. And to the benefit—scholarly not financial—of the authors, who could pass gratis copies of their writings to colleagues elsewhere and thus build up their academic reputations. Monograph publication was then, and is now, more common to scientific institutes and museums than to universities. No other university known to the writer ever made publication of scholarly papers—usually but not always too long for journals—so easy and convenient for its faculty members.

This was, of course, a publication system based on that of continental, particularly German, universities, one that must have been familiar to Benjamin Ide Wheeler during his student days at Leipzig, Jena, Berlin, and Heidelberg. Although given its start when another professor of Greek, Martin Kellogg, was president, the system must have been just what Wheeler wanted, and it was he who took hold of the small beginning and quickly made it into what was surely the largest monograph program in America.

We might remember that California was a young University: isolated on the Pacific coast, founded in 1868, moved from Oakland to Berkeley in 1873, it experienced its first great expansion after the turn of the century. It was also set down in a new land, not yet known in detail by scientists. There was much to examine and describe—geological features, plants, animals, insects. The anthropologists found Indian tribes living in the old way, speaking native languages still unstudied and unrecorded. And historians soon began to discover the little-known story of their own region. The monograph series provided what must have seemed—except perhaps to the historians—an ideal way to publish their research papers, long and short.

The individual monographs, ranging from a few leaves to several hundred pages each, were issued at irregular intervals and distributed in paper covers as they were printed. Complete volumes, with continuous paging for each volume, generally ran to about four hundred pages.

In 1893 the Committee on Publications had chosen as the generic title University of California Studies, but in 1901 the Editorial Committee changed this to University of California Publications, and those originally issued under other titles were eventually brought into conformity. But this title, an awkward one for daily use, is more than a little ambiguous, and it soon became common to speak of the Scientific Publications to distinguish them from administrative bulletins and other kinds of nonscholarly works under control of the Committee. When the Press began publishing books, the Committee called the monographs the Scientific Series. The term has continued in use to this day, although it has never appeared on the works themselves.

The original imprint of 1893 read, "Berkeley, Published by the University." In 1902 this was changed to "Berkeley, the University Press," a form found earlier on University official publications. It might have lived on if it had not been rejected by the United States Patent Office. In 1908 the office informed Albert Allen, the first manager of the Press, that names having geographical significance could not be registered by the agency. A year later, on 15 September, Allen reported this decision to the regents. No later correspondence on the subject has survived but the Editorial Committee (or the regents) soon adopted the form "University of California Press," with Berkeley, the place,

either preceding or following. Presumably no further attempt at registration was made.

The monograph Press was not only Wheeler's in spirit but
also his in daily deed. Although he sat for only one year as
chairman of the Committee on Publications—as Kellogg
had done before him—and although he did not attend
meetings, he participated by means of correspondence and
by interviews with members and after 1905 with Manager
Allen, and always exercised the right to approve or disap-
prove all actions taken. He appointed the members as he
appointed members of all other faculty committees,
thereby eliminating at the outset what he may have considered troublesome opposition. Members were reluctant
to decide important matters when the president was absent
from the University, postponing action until after his return.

Throughout his administration Wheeler kept a constant
watch on matters large and small. He approved regulations
concerning charges for authors' corrections. He allowed
authors additional free copies when the Committee would
not have granted them. He insisted that review copies, accompanied by résumés, be sent to his office to be for-
warded from there all at the same time. He gave final approval for hiring and firing and set the salaries of
stenographers and proofreaders. He determined the loca-
tion of the Press office and even assumed the role of interior
decorator, complaining on one occasion that a filing cabinet
was "not in harmony with the rest of the office furniture."

Wheeler decided whether authors were eligible to submit to the Press, pressured Editorial Committee members to approve manuscripts, and even submitted manuscripts on behalf of authors. He determined where works were to be printed and decided whether there would be extra shifts at the printing office to catch up with back work. He even concerned himself with book design. Displeased with the typography of a work, he wrote, "It makes it look as if we were trying to pad the book to make as much as possible out of our materials. It therefore has an ungenuine look to say nothing about its clumsy disagreeableness."

More important than these details, perhaps, was Wheeler's determination to preserve the "purity" of the Press. The only publications permitted were scholarly monographs in series, works for the most part given away rather than sold. He was vigorously opposed to policies or practices associated with commercial publishing. Books, by nature, were commercial. And of course he would not allow the payment of royalties or the use of advertising except for straight title listings; nor would he permit reprints, textbooks, or scholarly volumes of general interest. The one great exception was an unusual series to celebrate the fiftieth anniversary of the University, one that included a number of interesting and salable books, but most of these were primarily issued by other publishers, with the Press buying a few copies of each with its own imprint. Ironically, this project appears to have aroused the interest of some faculty members in a book program.

Although the old publishing program was valuable to research scholars and useful to the University, the old Press was what August Frugé has called a service agency rather than a publishing house.[6] Manager Allen had similar views. The series, taken together, became a kind of house organ, since only people connected with the University were eligible to submit manuscripts. That restriction, together with the shunning of all commercial or semi-commercial practices, made it impossible to convert the old program into a publishing house that would appeal to the writers of books, even writers on the home campus. One had eventually to be built up alongside it. But that was not soon. Wheeler's Press, operated by the Editorial Committee, persisted with little change for fourteen years after his retirement, and his publishing program flourished long after that.

6. "The Service Agency and the Publishing House," *Scholarly Publishing* (Toronto; January 1976): 121–27.

CHAPTER 4

THE EDITORIAL
COMMITTEE'S PRESS

When PRESIDENT WHEELER RETIRED in 1919 after twenty years of autocratic rule, faculty members were quick to begin their fight for some voice in university government. It is not surprising that the "revolt" took place in the six months between the time of Wheeler's retirement and the accession of the next president. The "revolutionaries" won for the faculty greater responsibility in the appointment and dismissal of colleagues, in the formulation of the budget, and in the internal conduct of the Academic Senate. The senate began choosing its own presiding officers and elected a committee on committees to appoint the members of faculty committees, including Editorial. Effective control of the University Press passed to the Editorial Committee and remained there until 1933.

The Editorial Committee antedated the Press by eight years, having been first appointed in 1885 to edit the *Register* and other administrative and academic announcements. Twelve years later it took charge of the *University of California Chronicle*, a new journal that was in large part a record of university life. When in 1901 the Committee became responsible for the research monographs, superseding President Kellogg's old Committee on Publications, it gained some measure of control over all classes of University publications. From 1905 to 1918, during Wheeler's time, there was a nonacademic manager of the Press; thereafter, until the Sproul-Farquhar reorganization in 1933, the managers were members of the Editorial Committee. The Committee was, in effect, the Press.

Appointed by the Academic Senate, the Committee derived its powers from that body. In the senate by-laws of June 1923 are spelled out powers, duties, and membership:

> The Editorial Committee shall consist of at least seven members of the Academic Senate. The Committee is charged, provisionally, with the publication of the University Register, of the University Chronicle, and of papers prepared by members of the faculty, and by graduate or other advanced students. The Committee is charged with supervision of all official publications of departments, colleges, schools, or other organized parts of the University. The Committee shall have the authority to determine the use of the title "University of California Press." The Editorial Committee shall report to the Academic Senate at least once a year.

The number of members remained nearly constant from 1901, when the Committee took over the monographs, until 1933—most often seven and never more than nine. Although appointments were made for one year only, most members served three or four years or even longer. At first the Committee met at irregular intervals, but beginning in 1914 it held regular semimonthly meetings. The secretary kept notes, which became the Minutes of the Editorial

Committee, an invaluable record that has continued to this day, recording policy decisions, action on manuscripts, and sometimes important discussion. The Minutes show that the Committee carried on its work according to a rather rigid set of principles, which were codified from time to time in a book of rules, first printed in 1908.

The *Rules of the Editorial Committee* was divided by type of publication: administrative bulletins, scientific publications, the University *Chronicle*, and library bulletins. The largest section was devoted to the so-called Scientific Publications, the series monographs. (The adjective "scientific" merely meant scholarly.) There were detailed regulations for all steps of the publishing process from the submission of manuscripts to the distribution of finished works.

The *Rules* changed very little in spirit, style, or content from 1908 to 1930, when the last version was printed before the reorganization of 1933. In the 1917 edition there were detailed regulations on author eligibility, previously set forth in the minutes. Eligible authors, in addition to faculty and students, included those commissioned to write papers to supplement research conducted at the University or to work on material owned by, or about to be donated to, the University. This definition of eligibility was held firmly ever after in relation to the Scientific Series and to the use of the Scientific Account, the Committee's annual appropriation. It did not apply to books published on risk funds or to journals, two categories that became important later.

From the beginning, series manuscripts came up to the Editorial Committee (or the Committee on Publications before 1901) from faculty editors or editorial boards for each series, but the Editorial Committee reserved the right to make final decisions about publication, a right that it has defended and retained for a great many years.

At first there were single faculty editors, Andrew Lawson for Geology, as we have seen, and Elmer Ellsworth Brown of the Department of Pedagogy for the University of California Studies, later called Education. But a subject series might embrace a number of subdisciplines and thus demand more expertise than any one person could provide and, beginning in 1908, the shift was made to boards of several members each. Boards also served to minimize the danger of undue lenience or harshness among colleagues—friends or enemies—a problem that would never go away but that could be controlled by the Editorial Committee.

In the old and still-small University it was natural enough for departments to take a proprietary interest in the series that published their research. They contended, and not without reason, that in the minds of scholars elsewhere a series would be identified with the department and that the department's reputation was at stake. The opposite danger, of course, was that a series might become, or become known as, a mere house organ rather than a place to publish the best research available. So there arose a tension between the boards and the Editorial Committee, one that persisted until in the 1970s the boards were abolished and replaced by panels of readers, less formally organized (see Appendix 1).

Although some efforts were made to publish books (see Chapter 5) and although the Editorial Committee members now made policy and managed editing, production, and distribution, the University Press retained the character imprinted so deeply by Benjamin Ide Wheeler. The twenty-three old monograph series flourished; some new ones sprang up. In the first forty years of the Press, from 1893 to 1933, there were published more than 2,000 separate papers in thirty-three subject series, totaling more than 100,000 printed pages.[1]

By 1913 it must have been thought—Wheeler must have thought—that the basic disciplines, or at least those that could make good use of series publication, had been provided for; no new series were established for almost ten years. But from 1921 to 1933, when the Press was reorganized, ten new series began publication. Only one of these, however, achieved real distinction and survived into later years.

A concise self-description appeared in the first volume, published in 1932: "The series Ibero-Americana is to form a collection of studies in Latin American culture, native and transplanted, pre-European, colonial, and modern."

---

1. Preliminary pages not counted. Figures compiled from *Catalogue: University of California Press Publications, 1893–1943*.

In practice, the area covered proved more restricted. With some exceptions the studies concerned native cultures and their relation to the Hispanic invaders in Mexico and early California. The first editorial board was made up of three famous scholars—Herbert E. Bolton, Alfred L. Kroeber, and Carl Sauer—but it was Sauer, a great cultural geographer, who stayed on the board for twenty-five years and is said to have been its guiding spirit. He wrote, with Donald Brand, the very first monograph—*Aztatlán: Prehistoric Mexican Frontier on the Pacific Coast.*

But the most active authors over the years were Sherburne F. Cook, a physiologist; Woodrow Borah, professor of history; and Lesley Byrd Simpson, professor of Spanish. Although their backgrounds differed, all were brilliant and original historians. Especially notable in the series were their many studies of the population of central Mexico in the colonial period; Cook, in addition, produced a group of controversial essays entitled *The Conflict Between the California Indian and White Civilization.* Other writers contributed archaeological, geographical, and economic studies.

This kind of interdisciplinary series, varied but with a decided character of its own, can probably flourish only if managed by a close-knit group of scholars with similar ideas, a sort of school rather than a group of disparate individuals. This relationship, as well as the pioneering quality of the work done, was recognized in France as early as 1960, when the noted historian Pierre Chaunu, of the Annales school, published a thirty-page review article entitled

"Une histoire hispano-américaine pilote: En marge de l'oeuvre de l'École de Berkeley."[2] Chaunu wrote in detail about the group's new methods of research in historical demography and about the significance of its work for understanding what happens when two civilizations come together. Much is gained by the interdisciplinary approach, he said; "Rarely . . . have interdisciplinary methods been used to such grand effect." And, in a final tribute: "From now on, the vigorous team from *Ibero-americana* has acquired a strong claim to the gratitude of all historians."

Chaunu wrote that the work of this remarkable group was too little known, perhaps because of the monographic mode of publication. Indeed, as the monographs became better known in this country, there was need for wider distribution, and in 1976 Cook's essays on the California Indians were collected and reprinted as a paperback book, along with a posthumous volume on the same subject, *The Population of the California Indians, 1769–1970*. The demographic studies of Cook and Borah, together with some new pieces, were published by the Press as *Essays in Population History* (3 volumes, 1971–79).

The more than fifty volumes of Ibero-Americana represent monograph publication at its best, but it is now clear that the series has nearly run its course, with only Borah of the main group still alive and writing. And the special circumstances, the accident of scholars coming together with a common intention, are not apt to be repeated soon.

2. *Revue Historique* (October–December 1960): 339–68.

For more than thirty years, the Editorial Committee had charge of a publication quite different in nature from the monograph series, the *University of California Chronicle*.[3] Begun in 1898, the year before the arrival of Wheeler, it continued until 1933. It was funded by the administration, not on the Committee's budget.[4]

When the regents authorized the new journal in late 1897, their minutes defined its scope in this manner: "It is expected to contain a record of the important events in University life, with noteworthy addresses on public occasions. It is much needed for exchange with other universities." Exchange was probably of first importance to Joseph Rowell, busy building up the library collection, but the contents of the *Chronicle* were directed not to other institutions or to outsiders of any kind but to members of the University community: faculty, students, and staff. The University Record, a regular feature, reported on local happenings. In a single issue in 1913 the Record included nearly twenty items: faculty appointments, promotions, leaves of absence; gifts to the University; the celebration of Mrs. Hearst's birthday; the president's biennial report; graduate enrollment; plans for University Extension; and much else. Important public addresses were printed verbatim, along with literary and scientific articles written in

3. The full title was changed several times, but in University circles it was generally known as the *Chronicle*.
4. The *Chronicle* was the only journal published before the late 1930s. Another journal, *Zoe* (1890–1908), although listed in the 1893–1943 *Catalogue*, appears to have been a private publication, later turned over to the Press for distribution.

a popular style by some of the more distinguished members of the faculty, such as Josiah Royce, Martin Kellogg, and G. H. Howison. The very first piece in the first issue was "The True Idea of a University" by Joseph LeConte, then nearing the end of his distinguished career.[5]

In its early years, and perhaps later, the *Chronicle* must have been a happy and useful publication to Berkeley people and to all connected with the University, but it was local in intention and not of wide interest. Like other journals that have survived into a changing world, it seems to have run its course and lost its purpose. As early as 1913, the editor of the *Chronicle*, Herbert E. Cory, professor of English, wrote to a member of the Editorial Committee: "The University of California Chronicle has been and is a curious and rather grotesque publication." An odd remark by an editor about his own journal, but it appears that Cory meant to say that the several parts of the journal were incongruous and "irreconcilable"—serious and attractive articles mixed in with odds and ends, trivia, and some rather bad original verse. It should be added that Cory aspired to edit a scholarly quarterly. Efforts to start a new journal like the *Yale Review* came to nothing then or later, and the *Chronicle* continued in pretty much the same fashion throughout Wheeler's regime.

After Wheeler, in 1921, the elimination of the subtitle

5. The LeConte brothers, Joseph and John, were among the first faculty members hired in 1868. In 1937 the Press published Joseph LeConte's *'Ware Sherman: A Journal of Three Months' Personal Experience in the Last Days of the Confederacy.*

An Official Record reflected a change in editorial policy. Doing away with the local character of the journal, the editors made an unsuccessful attempt to convert it into a magazine with wider appeal. This they did on a trial basis. By the early 1930s Manager George Calhoun and members of the Editorial Committee considered it a failed experiment and concluded, for both intellectual and financial reasons, that it should be discontinued. They felt that high standards were difficult to maintain without recompense to authors and that the poor distribution did not warrant the expense to the University. Sales were minimal, and the cost of sending the journal to institutions on the exchange list was greater than the estimated value of material received in return. Losses were heavy in depression dollars—$2,000 annually over a five-year period. In fall 1932 President Robert Gordon Sproul and members of the Editorial Committee unanimously agreed to discontinue publication.[6]

All in all, considering its uneven quality and the diversity of its contents over the years, the *Chronicle* was indeed a "curious" publication, as Cory described it. In hindsight, however, it remains one of the most accurate and detailed sources for the history and development of the University of California for the period that corresponds to the presidency of Benjamin Ide Wheeler.

6. Minutes, 2 December 1932 and 13 January 1933. Monroe Deutsch to Sproul, 11 July 1930 and 1 September 1932; Administrative Committee on the University Chronicle, 1 October 1932; Luther A. Nichols to Sproul, 1 November 1932; in Presidents' Files, Bancroft Library (Archives). Unless otherwise noted, correspondence and related documents cited henceforward are from the Presidents' File.

If, as we have been told, the camel was designed by a committee, it was a better job than the old story would allow,
given the special nature of the work to be done. And if the
Editorial Committee was the Press for the first forty
years—although dominated by Benjamin Ide Wheeler for
half that time—it must be said that it did an effective job
of managing the very specialized monograph program. A
committee might not be able to operate a genuine publishing house, with its daily problems, but it could and did
control the numerous University series.

In the very early years the few publications were handled by Joseph Rowell, the University librarian, and by
the Editorial Committee members in their spare time, but
after the great expansion under Wheeler this was no longer
possible, and the first manager of the Press, Albert Allen,
was hired in 1905. Allen was not a faculty member but an
1898 graduate of the University, a scholar of classical literature with a gift for writing. His talents were known to
C. M. Bakewell, professor of philosophy and chairman of
the Committee, who offered him the job at $900 per year.
Allen held out for $1,200, the amount he was earning at a
job in Visalia and, with some reluctance, Wheeler approved that amount.

During his twelve years at the Press, Allen not only did
most of the copyediting but also screened manuscripts for
the Editorial Committee, for whom he acted as secretary.
He also dealt with printers, both University plant and outside firms, and handled distribution to departments, exchanges, and sales. Most of this he had to do himself, since

Albert Allen. Graduation picture, 1898, seven
years before he became first manager of the
Press. Courtesy University Archives, The
Bancroft Library.

the University was niggardly in allowing the needed assistants or in paying enough to keep them. Once, in late 1908,
in answer to Allen's request to raise a clerk's salary, the secretary of the regents wrote: "It seems to me that it ought to
be possible to get a thoroughly satisfactory man to do the
work at $4.00 a week, the price we now pay provided we
fire a man often enough."

When Allen, who was dissatisfied with the provincial
nature of the Press, left to enter the army in 1917, he was
succeeded by Morse A. Cartwright (1917–24), but Cartwright had other duties in the president's office, seldom
showing up at the Press. So beginning in 1918 a succession

of faculty members served as secretaries of the Editorial Committee and managed the activities of the Press. The first of these (1918–19) was Monroe E. Deutsch, professor of classics, who later became provost and vice president of the University. He was replaced, briefly again, by Clarence I. Lewis, professor of philosophy, and then by Oliver Miles Washburn (1919–23), assistant professor of Latin and Greek.

After Washburn came George Miller Calhoun (1924–33), professor of Greek and member of the Editorial Committee, the last and most effective of the faculty managers. When he was on leave in 1928 he was spelled by Ivan Linforth, another professor of Greek.[7] It was the two of them who, several years earlier and shortly after Wheeler, had transformed the Sather chair of classical literature from a mere visiting professorship to a public lectureship with promise of publication. Calhoun, like Allen before him, had ideas about changing the nature of the Press, as we shall see in the next chapter.

In 1905 the Press office was located in North Hall, one of the first buildings on campus, no longer standing. It was moved to California Hall, then newly completed, but two years later the space was wanted for administrative offices, and the Press went in 1910 to the Bacon Art and Library Building, another structure since demolished, and in the

---

7. One may notice that the Press was dominated, from Kellogg and Wheeler through Calhoun, by professors of classics, particularly professors of Greek. So indeed was the University administration for much of the time.

following year to the new Doe Memorial Library. There it stayed until 1916, when the stock was transferred to Sather Tower and the office to the new printing building on Barrow Lane.[8] Thus began an uneasy cohabitation that continued, in two buildings, for forty-six years, sixteen of them as a single department.

The first handwritten "Rules of the Committee on Publications" in 1893 authorized the secretary to solicit printing bids—a clear indication that at the beginning the University plant did not do the work. The very early monographs in geology were done at the Pacific Press Publishing Company in Oakland.[9] The printing office, which antedated the Press by almost twenty years, was barely able to keep up with the printing of official publications, its primary task. The state printing office in Sacramento did some work for the University, but by the mid 1890s it was refusing work, a step that led the regents to threaten legal action in 1896 and to consider developing the plant on campus. The print shop was expanded the following year, but it was not until 1902 that it was able to take on scholarly work in addition to administrative printing.

8. Storage was a continuing problem. Publications were almost inaccessible in Sather Tower, wrote Albert Allen to the president. As late as 1950, remembers August Frugé, books and monographs were stored in half a dozen places around the campus, including under the seats in Edwards Stadium, where the rain came in on them. Eventually the stock had to be taken off campus.
9. Annual Report of the Secretary of the Board of Regents, 30 June 1893, p. 56.

For the next thirty years or more, as shown by the Minutes of the Editorial Committee and surviving correspondence, there was an almost-constant tension between the Committee or manager and the printers. The print shop was expanded again in 1907 and still again in 1916, in the new building on Barrow Lane, but could not keep up with both administrative work and scholarly publications. Again and again the latter piled up; delays extended to sixteen months in 1915, and Albert Allen reported to the president that there were forty-nine papers on the calendar, ranging in length from a few pages to several hundred; some of these were left over from the previous year.

Many times the Editorial Committee urged further expansion of the printing facilities. And it complained that Joseph Flinn, University printer (1887–1932), did not have the type necessary for specialized scholarly work, particularly in mathematics. From time to time the Committee and the manager moved to make use of outside printers, especially the New Era Printing Company in Lancaster, Pennsylvania, and even more especially when they began to suspect that outside work might be less rather than more expensive.

There was another problem at the University plant: Flinn's work was plain and serviceable but not pleasing to the eye, lacking any aesthetic quality. Publications that demanded better treatment had to be manufactured elsewhere. In the early 1930s, as Flinn's retirement grew near after forty-five years on the job, Editorial Committee members and Manager Calhoun began to think of a reorganized

The University printing office in 1893, located in the Mechanic
Arts Building annex. Courtesy University Archives, The Bancroft
Library.

print shop that could do more attractive work. In his recommendations to President Sproul, Calhoun asked that the
printing office be expanded to permit the printing of fine
books in the Harvard and Princeton tradition. In 1932
Samuel T. Farquhar, bibliophile and partner in the printing firm of Johnck and Seeger, was appointed superintendent of the printing office, and a year later—as will be
seen—he was made manager of the University Press.

Faculty editors or boards, then as later, concerned themselves primarily with the contents of manuscripts and with
their presentation in a general way, but not especially with

the niceties of printing style, which is the province of subeditors, as they are known in Britain, or copyeditors, as they are called in the United States. As manager from 1905 to 1917, Albert Allen did the copyediting almost single-handedly and without complaint from authors or Committee, a considerable achievement, considering the troubles that came later. There is no evidence that he ever changed an author's meaning for stylistic reasons, a fault charged against some of those who followed after him.

The Editorial Committee asked Allen to draft a manual of style, and just before he left the Press he found time to write *Suggestions on the Preparation of Manuscript*, in which he summarized the editorial wisdom accumulated during his twelve years of service. *Suggestions*, printed and used for many years, was intended, he said, primarily for inexperienced writers but might also be useful to older hands. Among other things he recommended that authors be concise but not carry this to an extreme that would make the text difficult to read. He also expressed an opinion that would endear him to many later directors and some editors—that if a paper required a great deal of rewriting, the author should be asked to pay for it.

Complaints appear to have been common in the years that followed Allen's departure. On one occasion in 1921 Manager Oliver Washburn wrote to Robert Gordon Sproul, then working in a business office, and asked that a bill for corrections sent to an author be canceled. It seems that a new copyeditor, since fired, had rewritten parts of the paper, already set in type, and—said Washburn—had mutilated them. Most of the changes had to be restored at considerable expense.

But Washburn did not always side with University authors. On one occasion the great anthropologist Alfred Kroeber complained about changes in a manuscript (not his own) that stultified the author's meaning. Washburn replied, in part: "You are of course aware that many contributors to our publications belong in the class of illiterates, and that a large amount of editorial revision is necessary if standards are to be maintained." Many a copyeditor since then has echoed this opinion but not always in public. Washburn did not say why such manuscripts were approved in the first place and not simply sent back for revision.

Complaints about copyediting seem to have subsided during the twelve years, after 1920, that Emily Wilkie served as editor. Managers from Allen to Calhoun, members of the Committee, and a number of authors seem to have thought highly of her work, but this opinion did not carry over to Calhoun's successor, Samuel T. Farquhar. Even before Farquhar took over as manager, he asked that Wilkie be demoted to editorial assistant, and he appointed Harold A. Small editor. In spite of Small's great skill, complaints arose again, and more than once, causing serious trouble between the Committee and the Press.

Distribution of the monographs was effected by exchange, by gift through departments and authors, and sometimes by sale. Exchange was the most efficient method and the most advantageous to the University, since it accomplished the double purpose of displaying the University's research in the educational institutions of America and Europe and enabling the Berkeley library to build up its collection of scholarly material from those regions. Throughout the forty years of the monograph Press, the exchange program was paramount; it remained important for a long time afterward and is still used to a lesser extent.

The librarian Joseph Rowell began making exchanges in the 1880s but had little to send out and called for a publishing program that would provide more and better materials. In the early years it was he who managed exchange and other distribution, but control later reverted to the Editorial Committee and to Manager Allen, who conducted correspondence, kept a list of names, and sent out new publications. When Allen left in 1917 there was agitation to shift the work to the library, but the change was slow and partial, and it was not until after 1950 that the Press simply told the library to manage a program that benefited it.[10]

The benefit was always great but not easy to quantify. A report for the years 1893–1907 showed that the library had received materials worth from $45,000 to $50,000, more than was spent on manufacturing the series papers. In the early 1930s another study reported similar results. And in later years it was estimated that the several Uni-

10. Information from August Frugé, who says he made the move.

versity libraries received annually more than $100,000
worth of materials in exchange for the monographs (see
Appendix 1).

The library in Berkeley, being first on the ground, received the greatest benefit, even in later years when an effort was made to give even treatment to Los Angeles and
the other campuses. It is generally agreed among librarians
that the extraordinary strength of the Berkeley collection
of foreign serials came about largely because of the exchange program. But there was no particular benefit to the
Press as a press; it served others but did not develop as a
publishing organization.

Free distribution was also generous. There was an "administrative" list that included institutions in California
and the west as well as individuals nominated by the president and others. University departments were allowed approximately one hundred and sometimes more copies of
papers written by their faculty members. These could be
used for departmental exchanges with departments elsewhere. And authors were allowed a varying number, from
fifty to two hundred copies, which they could send to colleagues at other institutions.

The University was also generous to troubled libraries
in other parts of the world. A full set of publications was
sent to the Biblioteca Nazionale in Turin, which had suf-
fered heavy losses through fire. And after the First World
War gifts were made to the universities of Louvain and
Lille, whose collections had been damaged, and offers were

made to other universities in France and Belgium that had incurred losses and had little money for replacement.

It is difficult to sell something that is also being given away. And the series monographs, with a few exceptions, were highly specialized and not of general scholarly interest. Since the income from sales was of no help to the Press but went into the general University fund, there was little or no incentive to mount an active selling effort. When Joseph Rowell was in charge of sales, his first annual report for 1893–94 showed a grand total of $42.05 received for the Geology and Education papers published that year. His best year, 1896–97, brought in $370.25, most of it from paid subscriptions to the first Geology volume.

The Editorial Committee, which took over from Rowell, left no useful record of sales until the time of Albert Allen, who kept a fairly consistent set of ledgers from 1905 to 1917. Sales passed the $1,000 mark in 1910–11, largely from a big volume on labor relations by Lucille Eaves and from Willis Linn Jepson's *Silva of California* in the Memoirs, an interdisciplinary series for works that required the quarto format. Receipts fell to $775.76 in 1912–13 but almost doubled in the following year when another volume in the Memoirs series, Wesley C. Mitchell's *Business Cycles*, became available. This was a classic work, later reprinted as a book.

Complete volumes such as Mitchell's turned out to be more salable than anything else until the books of the Semicentennial series came along in 1918. After Wheeler's retirement the publication of a few independent volumes (known as separate works) brought the figures up, so that 1922–23 saw a record high, before 1933, of over $11,000, when three of these separate works—including Eugene McCormac's *James K. Polk: A Political Biography*—were issued in one year. In 1932–33, just before the advent of the new regime, sales fell to $6,000.[11]

In spite of the poor prospects, some efforts were made to advertise or at least to serve notice of new publications. These were listed in *Minerva, Jahrbuch des Gelehrten Welt*, and later in *Publishers' Trade List Annual*. And in 1909 Allen began taking a quarter page twice a month in *Science*, a practice that continued into the 1940s, although it seems likely that the ad attracted as many requests for free copies—from departments and authors—as it did sales.

Efforts were made also to sell through agents of one kind or another in this country and abroad. Some series were entrusted to the great scholarly bookseller Otto Harrassowitz in Leipzig and others to R. Friedlander in Berlin. Some sales were made through book jobbers in this country, such as Baker and Taylor, Charles Scribner, A. C. McClurg, and Brentano's. In 1916 the Press joined with other university publishers, notably Harvard and Yale, in a sort of cooperative in New York, called the University Press Association. The results were not impressive for the old reasons together with a special one: the Press could not

11. The figures are taken from the reports of the secretary and treasurer of the regents and include only sales of publications funded on the annual appropriation and not those done on special funds.

supply the association with invoice forms because it had none. All business transactions had to go through the comptroller's office with remittances made in the name of the regents. This was not the last time that bureaucrats in other offices of the University made it nearly impossible for the Press to conduct business in an orderly fashion. August Frugé tells of jurisdictional battles that were still being fought out in the 1950s, and even in the 1960s.

By 1923 the association was no longer in business, but in that year the Press acquired a far more prestigious affiliation, one with Cambridge University Press for Great Britain and Ireland. Stock was at first consigned to Cambridge and later was sold at a 50 percent discount. The Cambridge imprint, along with the California one, was put on all publications for the next forty-five years; in 1968 the arrangement was discontinued by mutual agreement. By that time the Press had undergone two character changes and had become a book publisher.

CHAPTER 5

EARLY ATTEMPTS
AT BOOK PUBLISHING

IN THE FORTY YEARS THROUGH 1932 the number of separate books issued by the Press was twenty-seven, along with eight Semicentennial volumes and nine Sather lectures, both described below.[1] This came to a little more than one per year before 1933, compared to an annual average of more than fifty series monographs in the same years. Even after Wheeler's twenty-year interdiction, when some members of the Editorial Committee wanted to publish books and made rules in favor of them, they had no support from the administration, no regular funds but the annual series appropriation, and no way to attract authors. The Press remained a monograph press. Books were occasional, issued with special funds, or even accidental. But a description of them will suggest what might have happened under a more liberal president.

---

1. The discussion of books here and throughout this history includes only those published as separate works and those issued in the several book series (Sather, Semicentennial, United Nations). Excluded are individual series monographs that were bound and sold as separates, except for a few that were later revised and brought out as new editions. Excluded also are works published elsewhere but distributed by the Press.

The very first nonseries publication, *The Book of the Life of the Ancient Mexicans*, came to the Press—or rather to the University—by what may be called an accident.[2] Only special circumstances, involving donors to the University, could have led Wheeler to go along with it. The author, Zelia Nuttall, was an honorary assistant in American archaeology in the Peabody Museum at Harvard, whose curator was Frederick Ward Putnam. Originally from San Francisco, Nuttall seems to have been a friend of Phoebe Apperson Hearst. When in 1901 a new department of anthropology was founded with a gift from Mrs. Hearst, Putnam became its first head (from a distance and part-time) and Nuttall a member of the advisory committee along with, among others, President Wheeler and the noted Columbia University anthropologist Franz Boas, another friend of Nuttall. It seems likely that this connection was useful two years later when Nuttall needed to publish her book quickly.

In early 1890, while doing research in Florence, Nuttall discovered in the Biblioteca Nazionale Centrale an anonymous Mexican codex of the mid sixteenth century, which has become known as the Codex Magliabechiano, after an early Italian collector who left it, along with the rest of his library, to his native city. This work, which describes the

<hr>

2. The *Catalogue . . . 1893–1943* lists two earlier volumes that were not published by the Press. F. B. Meek, *Geological Survey of California* (1864), was issued by the State of California four years before establishment of the University; *Observatory Atlas of the Moon* (1897) was a publication of the Lick Observatory.

Zelia Nuttall. 1879. Courtesy The Bancroft Library.

cults, ceremonies, and festivals of the Indians of central Mexico, contains handsome colored drawings by an Indian artist together with explanatory text, which Nuttall at first thought was the work of one or more Spanish friars but eventually attributed to a sixteenth-century scholar, Cervantes de Salazar.

After establishing her priority among scholars and obtaining permission from the Italian authorities to publish, Nuttall had a facsimile printed by chromolithography in 1892, arranged with the Peabody Museum for distribution, and announced a publication that was to include translation and commentary. Years passed while she worked on the commentary, but in the meantime she displayed her material at scholarly meetings and passed information to other researchers.

Some of these became impatient. In 1902 and again in 1903 an American named Joseph Loubat, sometimes known as the Duc de Loubat, wrote to Nuttall, saying that if she did not publish at once he would bring out his own edition.[3] But Nuttall's translation and commentary were not ready, although sixty-one pages had been set in type at the University Press, Cambridge, Massachusetts. Deciding to issue the facsimile first and the commentary later, Nuttall hastily wrote a preface and an introduction, which she had printed at the same place. And when the Peabody refused to take advance subscriptions for the book and pre-

---

3. See Elizabeth Hill Boone, *The Codex Magliabechiano and the Lost Prototype of the Magliabechiano Group* (Berkeley, 1983), 14.

𝕿𝖍𝖊 𝕭𝖔𝖔𝖐
of the
𝕷𝖎𝖋𝖊 𝖔𝖋 𝖙𝖍𝖊 𝕬𝖓𝖈𝖎𝖊𝖓𝖙 𝕸𝖊𝖝𝖎𝖈𝖆𝖓𝖘

CONTAINING AN ACCOUNT OF

THEIR RITES AND SUPERSTITIONS

AN ANONYMOUS HISPANO–MEXICAN MANUSCRIPT PRESERVED AT
THE BIBLIOTECA NAZIONALE CENTRALE,
FLORENCE, ITALY

REPRODUCED IN FACSIMILE WITH INTRODUCTION, TRANSLATION, AND COMMENTARY BY

ZELIA NUTTALL

PART I.—Introduction and Facsimile

UNIVERSITY OF CALIFORNIA
BERKELEY
1903

The first Press book.

sumably was not prepared with ready financing, she dropped it as publisher and turned to her friends at the University of California. Publication by the University was financed by the Fund for Archaeological Research in Mexico, set up for the Department of Anthropology by two wealthy ladies, Mrs. William H. Crocker and Mrs. Whitelaw Reid. They are acknowledged in the preface, which was signed in Coyoacán, Mexico, in September 1903.

Although dated that year, the book probably did not appear until early 1904. The volume is oblong like the original manuscript and bound in flexible leather. The facsimile, printed in Florence more than ten years before publication, is on heavy handmade French paper, while the twenty pages of preliminary matter were printed on a different paper in Cambridge. Binding was probably done in California. The cost of completion, $1,654.02, was not a small sum in those days, although it is not clear whether this included either the Cambridge printing or reimbursement to Nuttall for any of her earlier expenses.

There were only two hundred copies. Still surviving at the Press are the initial distribution lists, which show that more than a third of the copies were given away to the principals in the affair, to libraries, and to prominent individuals. Others were sold at $25, the equivalent of at least $200 or $300 today.

The imprint, perhaps given to the printer in haste by Nuttall herself, is simply "University of California," without mention of the Press, but the book is listed as a Special Volume in the very first catalog of Press publications, dated October 1904.[4] The price of $25 was for both parts, with the second said to be in press—reasonably enough since sixty-one pages were in type in Cambridge.

But those pages have disappeared and so have all Nuttall's notes and drafts for the translation and commentary.[5]

4. Reproduced in Appendix 2. Presumably the Editorial Committee was not asked to approve the publication in advance; Wheeler would not have thought this necessary.
5. Information from Nuttall's biographer, Ross Parmenter of Oaxaca, Mexico.

Although she lived another thirty years, until 1933, she never finished the work, which remained hanging for eighty years. In the Press files is a series of letters exchanged with Manager Allen between 1910 and 1915, with Nuttall promising quick completion and Allen growing more and more exasperated. By 1915 Nuttall had returned to California from a trip to Spain and did not feel free to go back to her home in Mexico because of the ongoing revolution.

What happened or did not happen after that is not clear from the Press records. Allen departed for the army in 1917, and the matter was presumably forgotten, even though purchasers were still entitled to another volume. In 1927 Emily Wilkie wrote about it to Alfred Kroeber, who told her that, in his opinion, Nuttall would never complete this book or any other. And indeed she seems to have been one of those scholars—a type well known to publishers— who are psychologically unable to finish their work.[6] She published Part 1, lacking the commentary, only when threatened by Loubat; in thirty years she did not finish Part 2; and she never produced the text to go with the planned publication of a 1550 map of Mexico City by Alonso de Santa Cruz. Four hundred facsimile copies of the map were stored in Berkeley for nearly seventy years until issued by the Museum of Anthropology in 1974.

---

6. Harold Small used to say—Frugé recalls—that no book is ever completed; it is only abandoned.

Eighty years after publication of Part 1, in 1983, the Press published a reproduction of the earlier book—a facsimile of the facsimile—together with a companion volume by Elizabeth Hill Boone of Dumbarton Oaks. Boone provides a translation of the Spanish and Nahuatl texts along with a detailed study of the codex and five other, similar manuscripts, all derived from a lost prototype.

No other books were published for almost twenty years, except those included in the Semicentennial series, a large undertaking designed to commemorate the University's fiftieth anniversary in 1918. The intention must have been to celebrate fifty years with fifty volumes, because the 1893–1943 *Catalogue*, meant to be complete but perhaps not entirely so, lists forty-eight titles. Of these seventeen were bound series papers and another twenty-three were books issued by other publishers, with the Press buying copies with its imprint—an indirect way of subsidizing the outside publisher. The Press copies of all volumes in the collection were bound in heavy blue cloth or buckram with a gold seal on the cover. Some were given away at the time of the celebration, others held for sale.

The remaining eight Semicentennial books appear to have been published by the Press alone. Given Wheeler's attitude about book publication, it seems possible that no outside publisher could be found for these few and that there was no choice but to bring them out solely with the Press imprint. One was a large and important book, *The Game Birds of California* (1918), by Joseph Grinnell, Harold

Child Bryant, and Tracy Irwin Storer, a contribution from the Museum of Vertebrate Zoology. A later companion volume by two of the same authors, Grinnell and Storer, *Animal Life in the Yosemite*, came out in the post-Wheeler period in 1924. Both are still sought by collectors, in part because of the fine colored reproductions of paintings by Allan Brooks.

Among the books that followed Wheeler's retirement in 1919 was one notable group, the Sather Lectures. Although these have sometimes been listed among the Scientific Series, they are really books and were financed by the Sather fund and not by the Editorial Committee's appropriation. The Sather professorship was established in 1912 with a bequest from Jane K. Sather, the widow of a wealthy banker who had come to California from Norway. It was a visiting professorship held each year by a distinguished scholar of Greek or Latin, who came to Berkeley, taught a course, and associated with students and faculty. But in 1920, when appointments were no longer made by Benjamin Ide Wheeler but by the departments of Greek and Latin, a transformation was engineered by two professors of Greek, George Calhoun of the Editorial Committee and Ivan Linforth. Henceforth, the visitor was asked to present a series of public lectures and to submit a manuscript based on them for publication by the Press.

Nine Sathers were brought out before 1933, among them books by such distinguished scholars as Herbert Weir Smyth of Harvard, John Linton Myers of Oxford, Tenney

Jane K. Sather. Portrait by William Keith, 1892. Courtesy University Archives, The Bancroft Library.

Frank of Johns Hopkins, and Martin Persson Nilsson of the University of Lund. This early book series is particularly worthy of note because it established a great tradition that is carried on to this day, with more than fifty volumes published. It is generally thought to be the most distin-

guished series of classical lectures in this country and perhaps anywhere. And it may be the greatest accomplish-
ment of the old Press in book publishing.[7]

Before this, the restrictions of the Wheeler years were
not pleasing to Albert Allen. Wishing to issue books of
general scholarly interest, even some of a semicommercial
nature, he applied for permission to visit and study some
of the major scholarly presses in the eastern part of the
country. Only reluctantly did Wheeler grant permission,
without pay and from November 25 to December 15,
barely enough time for a cross-country journey in 1914.
Allen visited the presses at Chicago, Harvard, and Yale,
and on his return requested an appointment to tell the president what he had learned. There is no evidence in the files
to show that Wheeler ever granted the appointment; probably he never did.

That his appeal fell on deaf ears must have been no surprise to Allen, but he did not put the matter out of mind.
In his Report of the University Press, 1915–16, which he
submitted to the president about a year before he left the
Press for the army in the summer of 1917, he caustically
and publicly criticized the Press and the president, charg-
ing that the publishing program, so limited in its scope,
served the selfish interests of the University community
rather than the interests of scholarship at large:

7. For a full account of this book series see Sterling Dow, *Fifty Years of
Sathers* (Berkeley, 1965). See also August Frugé, "Lectures into Books,"
Scholarly Publishing (Toronto; January 1981): 158–66.

The University of California Press is therefore not in the general publishing business. Except for a few instances it has not issued books. It is not, in fact, a "Press" in the meaning which the activities of other institutions have given the term "University Press." Through it the University of California has served only its own purposes; it has not yet been put at the service of scholars outside of the membership of this University.

. . . But the question will surely soon be raised whether . . . the University of California shall not, if and as it is able, extend the privilege of publication through its University Press to the work of others than its own members. . . . The number of books published would at first, and perhaps for several years, be very small. But a . . . Press continuing to grow upon this broad basis will testify, as no publishing department limited to the publications of the University's own work can adequately testify, to the care of the University for the search of Truth and for its dissemination.

One may speculate that the very first manager might have reformed the Press if he had been allowed to. As it happened, more than a generation passed before California could take its place alongside other university book publishers. Allen was never honored formally for his service or his ideas, but extant documents, such as the one just quoted, bear witness to his versatility, talent, and understanding of scholarly publishing.

In 1919, the year of Wheeler's retirement, the question of books came up once more. Members of the Editorial Committee, elated by the increase in receipts from the sale of the Semicentennial Publications and about to be liber-

ated from a repressive president, called for a book program
in their report for that year:

> A policy of accepting suitable contributions for publication
> as separate bound volumes seems desirable from two points
> of view: first, it would mean the building of a set of "list
> books" having a steady sale over a period of years; second, it
> would result in the identification with this University of a far
> larger portion of the scholarly productions of its faculty.

The final words imply clearly that faculty members preferred taking their larger, and perhaps more important,
work to other publishers, a condition that persisted for
many years.

There is no indication in the Minutes of the Editorial
Committee that Wheeler's successor, David Prescott Barrows (1919–23), made any answer, pro or con. The Committee took matters into its own hands. After study by a
subcommittee the full Committee voted "that works which
constitute complete volumes may, at the request of the author and of a duly appointed editor and at the discretion of
the Editorial Committee, be printed and bound in a form
resembling trade books of similar character." At first these
were referred to as independent volumes but later, and for
many years to come, they were called separate works. A set
of rules governing them was formulated in 1920 and appeared essentially unchanged in the printed *Rules* of 1924.
Books were not to be used for exchange but held for sale.
Authors were to receive twenty-five rather than two hundred gratis copies. The word "advertising" was mentioned.
Although nothing was said of funding, the Committee had

no money other than its annual state appropriation and could not very well have used this for books by authors not connected with the University. Nor, for the same reason, could it have paid royalties. The intentions were there; the means were not.

President Barrows neither sanctioned nor condemned the new policy, but he discouraged the acceptance of more book manuscripts beyond the three or four that were in the works by the time he got around to writing to the Committee in 1922. "We may be able," he wrote, "to judge from the success of these how much further we should go in this matter and whether we should, like the ordinary book publishing concern, seek good manuscripts instead of waiting for them to come to us." Many years would pass before the Press began to make an active search for manuscripts.

Barrows' successor, William Wallace Campbell (1923–30), must have felt the same way about book publishing. In spite of requests from the Committee, he would not formally approve a change in policy but did his best to evade the issue. So in April 1929 the Committee again took its own action to authorize provisionally the publication of textbooks of scholarly character, without royalty to authors; to consider book manuscripts by authors who were not faculty members; and to approve the reprinting of works whenever the ends of science would be served thereby. This brave and bold policy was seen by some, including Alfred Kroeber, as a threat to the Scientific Series. Kroeber need not have worried; the Committee had no investment funds at its disposal, nor were authors of salable books apt to give them to a publisher that paid no royalties. But the wish was there. Members of the Committee, perhaps without realizing the implications for their own powers, wanted a different kind of press.

During the late 1920s and the first years of the next decade from two to four books were published each year. They included the large works translated and edited by Herbert E. Bolton: Palóu's *Historical Memoirs of New California* (4 volumes; 1926), *Fray Juan Crespi* (1927), and *Anza's California Expeditions* (5 volumes; 1930). These handsome volumes, which from their appearance must have been printed outside Flinn's plant, were financed by Sidney M. Ehrman; they are still much sought after by collectors of western Americana.

Things began to change after Robert Gordon Sproul became president in 1930. In contrast to earlier presidents, Sproul was not a scholar. Granted a B.S. in civil engineering in 1913, he returned to the University a year later as cashier in the comptroller's office. By 1925 he was comptroller, secretary to the regents, and vice president in charge of business and financial matters, offices held concurrently until he was made president in 1930. During a six-month tour of other universities just before taking office, he is said to have been on the lookout for a new manager of the Press, an indication that he may already have thought of making the Press into something other than a part-time faculty activity.

The Editorial Committee appears to have felt that Sproul would be amenable to an expanded Press operation,

ANZA'S CALIFORNIA EXPEDITIONS

VOLUME I

AN OUTPOST OF EMPIRE

BY

HERBERT EUGENE BOLTON

PROFESSOR OF AMERICAN HISTORY AND
DIRECTOR OF THE BANCROFT LIBRARY
UNIVERSITY OF CALIFORNIA

UNIVERSITY OF CALIFORNIA PRESS
BERKELEY, CALIFORNIA
1930

and in the spring of 1930, just before the change of re-
gimes, Manager Calhoun (who was also a member of the
Committee) formulated recommendations for reorganization. In his accompanying letter to the president, Calhoun
wrote:

> Since our interview regarding the possibility of expanding
> the activities of the University Press, I have been giving
> much thought to the suggestions you have made and have
> discussed the project informally with members of the faculty
> who are particularly conversant with the problems involved
> in the publication of research. I am inclined to believe that
> the faculty of the University will strongly be in favor of ex-
> pansion provided (1) that it does not involve any lowering of
> standards; (2) that adequate provision can be made for the ex-
> pansion through an endowment to be contributed by friends
> of the University.

Calhoun asked that an endowment of not less than
$200,000, increasing over time to a maximum of $500,000,
be provided,[8] with the income to be used to "build up and
maintain an adequate sales organization and to defray the
expense of publication outside the established series, and
that the Regents of the University continue to make appropriations to cover the fixed expenses of the University
Press and the existing scientific publications." He asked
that a sales office be created, staffed by a sales manager and
an assistant in charge of advertising, to promote and sell
books both by direct mail and through retail book dealers.

8. This seems an unrealistic and impossible request, especially in 1930
dollars.

He recommended that royalties be paid in order to bring in books by well-known scholars outside the University and to prevent faculty authors from sending their money-making books elsewhere. The planned expansion would necessitate the use of bookkeeping methods customary in the trade, making advisable a separate accounting office. And of course proceeds from sales should be credited to the Press and not to the University's general funds.

As for organization, Calhoun proposed that the functions then performed by the manager of the Press be divided. The purely managerial ones would be passed to a sales manager, who would be responsible for the operating and financial administration, while relations with the president and the Academic Senate would be exercised by a member of the faculty, who would sit with the Editorial Committee and concern himself with such matters as the selection of manuscripts. His title might be general editor or director of University publications.

It would be difficult to judge Sproul's reaction to these proposals. For the time being he did nothing, as was often his practice, but in 1932 he appointed a special committee to advise on reorganization. Given the date, when Samuel Farquhar must have been waiting in the wings, this move may have been a token gesture to make the faculty feel good. The chairman of the special committee, Professor Arthur Brodeur, reported to Sproul in a letter dated 24 May 1932. It was not until some six months later that Sproul commented on the issues raised by the committee. By that time members must have surmised that the new

head of the Press would not be a member of the Editorial
Committee or the faculty.

To the special committee's recommendation that the
"chief function of the University Press will continue to be
the publication of the results of scholarly research and the
advancement of Knowledge," Sproul replied, "I agree
heartily." In answer to its plea that "nothing in the function
of the Manager shall be permitted to interfere with the duties and powers of the Editorial Committee," he simply
stated, "This is my understanding." But to the committee's
suggestion that "the total amount to be expended from the
appropriation for the University Press: Expense and
Equipment . . . should have the approval of the Editorial
Committee," the president retorted, "The suggestion as
phrased by your Committee would seem to be an encroach-
ment on the proper functions of the manager of the Press."
The committee's report concluded with questions that
seem more like expressions of apprehension than requests
for further information: "Is the Manager to be primarily a
printer? Or primarily a sales manager? Or a more ideal
type of officer with subordinates to carry out the functions
of printer and sales manager?" Sproul did not answer these
questions, but his statement on the "proper function of the
manager of the Press" should have made it quite clear that
this individual was to be more than printer or sales manager. The president closed his letter by firmly stating his
intention to recommend to the regents that Farquhar, the
new superintendent of the printing office, be appointed
manager of the Press. He did not seek the Committee's ad-

Samuel T. Farquhar. Ca. 1942.

vice or approval. He announced it as a fait accompli and further suggested that Farquhar's initiation as manager take place during the time that remained before he assumed the position officially in summer 1933.

The new manager was not responsible to the Editorial Committee but directly to the president for general matters and to the comptroller for financial concerns. He became involved in the work of the Press at once, when Calhoun asked him to take over the direction of the editorial office. And a few months later he changed the printing specifications for the series and told the Committee that he would seek its advice when he wanted to depart from established style, although he was not required to do so.

In spring 1933 Farquhar formulated his own recommendations, not very different from those of Calhoun, for the reorganization of the Press. One major difference was that he did not request a huge endowment; another, of course, was that the manager would not be a member of the faculty and would be much more than an office manager or sales manager. Although Farquhar sought the advice and approval of the Committee, he suggested that it would not control the book program as it controlled the series publications. Before taking his recommendations to the president, he discussed them with the Committee after writing as follows:

> I am submitting to the Editorial Committee for its advice certain proposals which I expect to make to the President. Although I believe these matters are beyond the jurisdiction of the Committee, I feel that the Committee should be kept informed of all matters concerning the Press. I also feel that they will be more readily adopted if they have the backing of the Committee.

So it came to pass that at two meetings held in April 1933, after some deliberation and discussion of the manager's right to participate in the approval of book manuscripts, Committee members voted, no doubt with some reluctance, to support these proposals. They thereby limited their own authority and played a role in ushering in a new order at the Press. But there were power struggles to come, and the Committee was to play a central role in them.

CHAPTER 6

THE REORGANIZATION
OF 1933

Marriage of Printing and Publishing

THE UNIVERSITY OF CALIFORNIA PRESS, in its first forty years, may be described as a faculty committee that issued scholarly monographs for gift and exchange distribution. When Samuel Farquhar became manager in 1933 there took place the first of the changes that eventually— nearly twenty years later—made the Press into a publisher of scholarly books distributed through ordinary trade channels. The Press and the Editorial Committee became two separate entities, working—not always in harmony— toward the publication of series monographs and books, from the highly specialized to the somewhat popular. The Press assumed total responsibility for editing, manufacturing, and distributing as well as selecting books to be published on risk funds. The Committee's responsibilities were restricted to selecting manuscripts for publication on state funds and to confirming (or not) the scholarly and literary quality of manuscripts selected by the manager for publication on other funds. Though the manager and Committee members generally "coexisted," they engaged in battle on a number of occasions, when faculty members saw the newly established book program as a threat to the publication of series papers or as a limitation of their powers.

For the first time the Press and the printing office were joined in 1933 under Farquhar's management, with the printing office renamed the Printing Department of the University Press. It was Farquhar who suggested the union. He may have been an empire builder or he may sincerely have felt that the change would benefit both departments. Instead, since printing needs are often at odds with publishing needs, the union surely held back the development of the Press as a publisher. Farquhar the publisher was often forced to yield to Farquhar the printer, especially when there was an urgent need for administrative printing in the expanding University of the 1930s and 1940s. It seems clear, too, that he thought as a printer and not as a publisher. His efforts to improve and expand the print shop, though praiseworthy and successful, could not keep pace with the ever-increasing demands placed upon it, nor in the long run was it possible to maintain the competitive prices needed by a publisher. Viewed in retrospect, the combination of the Press and the printing office was an interlude in the long history of the Press. In California, as in most other universities, separation became necessary.

The years of transition—between the old monograph Press and the modern Press—extend beyond the death of Farquhar in 1949. The Press did not begin to develop as a publishing house of any stature until the marriage of the two departments was dissolved. The dissolution required stages; it was not accomplished without an intra-university fight that went on for several years. Although complete formal separation did not come until after President Sproul retired in 1958, by about 1952 or 1953 August Frugé was operating the Press in a way that was substantially independent of the plant. It was his reforms of the early 1950s that marked the true beginnings of the modern Press.

Samuel Thaxter Farquhar, born 10 May 1890 in Newton, Massachusetts, received a Bachelor of Arts degree from Harvard University and attended its School of Business Administration for a semester. After graduation he worked for a time as a financial reporter on the *Boston Herald* but soon left journalism for advertising and worked for several firms on both coasts between 1914 and 1920, when he became president of his own advertising firm, Farquhar and Seid. An interest in lettering led to an interest in typography and fine printing and led him also out of the advertising business. After a few years as a printing salesman, he went to work in 1926 for Johnck and Seeger, Printers, in San Francisco, and by the end of the following year became a full partner in the firm. John Johnck, a good master printer, and Harold Seeger, his partner, produced handsome work, known for its clean-cut quality and refined taste. Lawton Kennedy, a Bay Area printer of considerable repute, did the presswork for them. Johnck, Seeger, and Kennedy were influential in Farquhar's development as a book designer.

He soon became sufficiently expert to write a weekly
column on fine printing that appeared in the *San Francisco
Chronicle* in 1927 and 1928. Active in several clubs for de-
votees of the fine book, he was one of the founders of the
Roxburghe Club of San Francisco.[1] His reputation led
some members of the Editorial Committee to think of him
as a possible replacement for Joseph Flinn, the superintendent of the printing office, whose work was serviceable but
not handsome and who was due to retire in 1932. But it was
not the Committee that made the appointment. Francis
Farquhar, San Francisco accountant and author and
brother of Samuel, told the story this way.

Samuel, who was living in Berkeley while working at
Johnck and Seeger, commuted to San Francisco by train
and ferry. Unlike most commuters, he did not read mag-
azines, newspapers, or light fiction on the boat but instead
looked at the rare book catalogs of Maggs Bros. and read
the Latin classics. He attracted the attention of another
commuter of similar interests, James K. Moffitt. Moffitt, in
addition to being a collector of fine editions of Horace and
a reader of Maggs' catalogs, was a long-time and influential
member of the Board of Regents of the University. According to Francis, common interests led to friendship,
supper invitations to Moffitt's home, and Samuel's appointment first as superintendent of the printing office and

1. Hazel Niehaus to Chandler Grannis, *Publishers' Weekly*, 25 May 1949;
Johnck and Seeger, Printers, broadside, *The New Year, 1928*, in Press
files; Francis P. Farquhar, "Comments on Some Bay Area Printers," in
Edwin Grabhorn Interview Volume, Bancroft Library (Oral History).

shortly thereafter as manager of the Press. The appointments were discussed and settled at social gatherings and private interviews before they were officially announced. His appointment as manager of the Press seems to have come as a surprise to Calhoun and other faculty members who had planned a different kind of reorganization.

With limited experience as a printer and next to none as a publisher, Farquhar came to work with the backing of a powerful regent and thus of the president. Without this support, silent or otherwise, he might not have survived his battles with restrictive administrators and resentful faculty members, nor would he have been able to improve printing standards and expand the plant to the extent that he did.[2]

PRINTING

The printing plant existed to serve other University departments, which were in effect captive customers; printing bills, including a percentage for the building and equipment reserve, were paid by interdepartmental recharges. Because of its nonacademic character this department, unlike the Press, was organized under the comptroller's office, with the superintendent reporting directly to the comptroller.

When Farquhar took charge of the printing office he succeeded a man who had been in charge of the plant for forty-five years. His letters and reports to Comptroller Luther

2. Interview with Francis P. Farquhar, Berkeley, 27 March 1974; interview with Helen Leete Farquhar, Berkeley, 28 April 1974; *Press News*, December 1945, vol. 1, no. 6, p. 1.

A. Nichols contain both praise and criticism of his predecessor as well as a fair share of praise for himself. He
wrote in his first report:

> I pay tribute to Mr. Flinn's extraordinary ability to select ca-
> pable, willing assistants. The only possible criticism of the
> personnel is that they lack initiative, which can be under-
> stood when it is considered that Mr. Flinn was an autocrat,
> albeit a kindly one, and would brook no interference with his
> direction of affairs.[3]

He added that he "immediately made each foreman in the
shop responsible for his own department and at the same
time gave him authority commensurate with the responsibility." Farquhar reported that he had found the plant in
excellent condition with certain notable exceptions.

Reform began with the composing room, where the
foreman was demoted and replaced by Fred E. Ross,
brought over from Johnck and Seeger, who later became
Farquhar's collaborator in designing books. In his efforts to
achieve a clear and sharp impression of type on paper, he
replaced worn mats as well as long-reused type metal and
old foundry type for hand composition. He also objected
to the inferior paper then used in order to save money. On
this subject Farquhar was an expert; he demanded the best
and claimed rightly that he knew more about paper than
did the University's purchasing agents. Outraged at their
interference, he asked the comptroller to deliver him from
these bureaucratic nuisances and to declare him, in writ-

3. Farquhar to Nichols, Report, 4 August 1932, in Press files.

Joseph W. Flinn, University printer. 1930s.
Courtesy University Archives, The Bancroft
Library.

ing, sole arbiter in the choice of paper. This Nichols did in
December 1932.

Several months after becoming superintendent, Farquhar drew up new specifications for the printing of series
monographs. Discussing these with members of the Editorial Committee, he promised—as a matter of courtesy—
to keep them informed on contemplated changes in printing style but made it clear that he reserved the right to

make decisions on all such matters. Thus did he assert himself as the new typographical expert.[4]

Although improvements were substantial, the plant remained cramped in the Barrow Lane quarters and lacked equipment needed for scholarly work. Farquhar, like his predecessor, had to give precedence to administrative printing with its rigid deadlines. In reporting to the comptroller at the end of his first year, he congratulated himself on getting all departmental and administrative work out on time but anticipated complaints from authors of series monographs. So began the long campaign for a new plant, one that would, Farquhar believed, enable him to produce both administrative and scholarly works on schedule. In his report of three years later, he was even optimistic enough to claim that enlarged facilities would make it possible to take on printing for other institutions of higher education, earning profits that would make for lower prices within the University.[5]

For many years the University had been setting aside money to construct and equip a new building. By 1934, with the reserve amounting to $200,000, Comptroller Nichols felt that construction could start within a few years and he asked Farquhar to study the needs. The latter at once threw himself into drawing up plans and soon he was putting pressure on Nichols to rush their implementation. His reports between 1936 and 1938 contained an

4. Minutes, 2 December 1932.
5. Farquhar to Nichols, Reports, 9 June 1933, 12 July 1933, 15 September 1936, in Press files.

ever-growing litany of complaints about crowded conditions. His words to Nichols and others must have been effective, for in 1938 the regents approved the purchase of a piece of land at Oxford and Center streets, facing the west side of the Berkeley campus.

The building was completed and operating by December 1939. The cost, including new equipment, amounted to approximately $400,000, of which $250,000 came from the accumulated reserve while the remainder was provided by the Public Works Administration. The building, described in the early 1940s as conservatively modern in design, was meant to provide ample space for both the Press and the print shop. The plant, one story high, was under a single roof supported by widely spaced pillars, with movable partitions. Sawtooth skylights and the south wall of glass brick shut out direct sunlight and flooded the manufacturing area with a soft natural light.

The new plant was furnished with the latest equipment, including four new linotypes (Model 30 Blue Streak), sophisticated machines in their time that could cope with the intricacies of scholarly printing, which Farquhar felt were capable of producing a page that looked as if it had been hand set. Space was provided for offset presses but these never arrived during Farquhar's time, although he did hire a person to prepare offset copy for sending to other plants.

The front part of the building, three stories high, faced Oxford Street. On the top floor was a hand bindery that did work for the University libraries; immediately below were the sales and editorial offices of the Press; and on the

The printing office on Barrow Lane. 1922. Courtesy University Archives, The Bancroft Library.

The Oxford Street building, opened late 1939.

The Press staff, taken at the opening of the Oxford Street building, March 1940. Front row, left to right: M. L. Willard, assistant editor; D. C. Wilcox, junior clerk; H. Niehaus, secretary, University Press printing department; B. Baker, secretary; A. Hus, editorial assistant; E. Rice, stenographer, University Press; M. A. Whipple, editorial assistant; V. B. Smith, editorial assistant; K. Towle, assistant to the manager. Back row, left to right: W. A. Garrett, sales manager, University Press; H. A. Small, editor; V. J. McHenry, superintendent; J. W. Flinn, University printer emeritus; S. T. Farquhar, manager, University Press and printing department; M. J. Feak, foreman, retired, pressroom; J. A. D. Muncy, assistant superintendent.

ground floor the combined administrative offices, opening off the entrance lobby. Singled out for special praise was the spiral staircase of terrazzo running from the lobby to the second floor. Halfway up, a large window gave staff members and visitors a view of the plant in full operation below. Articles in national trade journals hailed the build-

Farquhar showing President Sproul the new Press at the
formal opening of the Oxford Street building. March 1940.

ing as one of the finest printing and publishing plants in the
country, both for comfort of workers and for efficiency of
work flow.[6]

But the new plant never did away with the old problems.
At the end of the first year of operation, Farquhar had to
face angry authors whose hope had turned to frustration.
Asked by the president's office to justify himself, Farquhar
said in defense of the plant and himself that the plant was
adequately equipped and capable of handling all University printing except during rush periods when most of the

6. *Printing Equipment Engineer* (January 1940): 11–14; *Western Construc-
tion News* (February 1940): 48–49.

machinery had to be used for administrative work.[7] This was a permanent and basic problem. If the shop were large enough to do both administrative and scholarly work during the rush months, it would be too large (and too expensive) the rest of the year.

During World War II paper rationing, lower budgets for series monographs, and the concentration of the book program on Japanese-language textbooks, printed offset by outside firms, lessened the demands on the plant. But afterward there came a tremendous increase in the volume of work, brought on by a huge jump in student enrollment and a proportionate growth in faculty. Complaints were renewed, not only in Berkeley but also in Los Angeles. President Sproul ordered an investigation, asking specifically whether a second plant should be established in Los Angeles or whether the University should contract with commercial establishments. The best solution, according to administrators in Los Angeles, was to buy from commercial firms in southern California.[8] Eventually Farquhar hired a printing consultant in Los Angeles (William Foley), who also set up a second library bindery.

In the late 1940s Farquhar appealed once more to Comptroller (later Vice President) James Corley, asking for more space and equipment and noting the pressure put on him by a group of faculty members. Corley and President Sproul ruled against expansion in favor of sending some of

7. Farquhar to Deutsch, 25 November 1940.
8. David L. Wilt to George F. Taylor, 17 January 1946; Taylor to James Corley, 28 January 1946; Farquhar to Sproul, 4 June 1947.

the work to outside printers.[9] But by the early 1950s Corley had done a turnaround; it was he who led the fight to forbid Press books from going to outside firms.

The high cost of printing had always been a concern. After the war, when printing wages doubled in a short time and costs shot skyward everywhere, the problem became particularly acute in Berkeley and especially in book publishing. Costs in western plants were generally higher than in the east, where specialized book plants could control a large volume of work and hold unit costs down. Edition binding was particularly high, done by hand in the west and by machine in the east.

High western costs posed a threat to the publishing part of the Press, since books had to be sold on a national market and could not be priced up to account for local conditions, as could general printing to captive customers. Farquhar was caught between the needs of the printing plant and those of his own publishing officers. He asked August Frugé, then associate manager, to prepare a report on publishing difficulties, brought on by high costs in the University plant and in other western shops, and how the Press was attempting to solve them. The hopes of the Press for survival in a national book market, said Frugé, depended on its ability to buy book manufacture on competitive bids, east and west. It could not survive as a captive customer. Farquhar sent the report on to President Sproul, endorsing

9. Corley to Farquhar, 25 August 1947; Farquhar to Corley, 26 August 1947; Corley to Sproul, 14 May 1948; Corley to Farquhar, 10 June 1948; Corley to Arnold Intorf, 14 September 1948.

informally a policy of competitive bidding. But the manager died not long afterward, and several years of contention followed.[10]

REORGANIZATION OF PUBLISHING

As noted earlier, Farquhar put together his proposals for reorganizing the Press, with the perhaps-grudging approval of the Editorial Committee, in April 1933, a few months before he took office as head of the newly combined Press and printing office. Since the president, Regent Moffitt, and he had already agreed on the general direction to be followed, it is not surprising that Sproul approved most of the recommendations, modifying or rejecting only a few.

The Press, it was agreed, would remain under the direction of the president, with authority over financial matters delegated to the comptroller, who was already in charge of the printing office. Farquhar would have liked the title of Director of the Press, but in the University scheme of things a directorship implied membership in the Academic Senate. (The title and membership were not granted until 1957.) As a kind of compromise, Sproul agreed to the title of Manager of the Press and University Printer.

Within the Press Farquhar proposed an expanded editorial department that could provide copyediting for Uni-

10. August Frugé, "Statement to the Editorial Committee on Publishing Problems," 26 February 1948 (mimeographed, in Press files and University Archives); Farquhar to Sproul, 31 March 1948.

versity authors, no matter where their books might be published, and also for the establishment of a sales department,
with the salary of the sales manager to be charged against
sales income. These proposals were approved, but there
never turned out to be enough editorial time for any but
Press publications. Farquhar also asked, but without success, that the University mailing division, part of the
comptroller's office, be put under his jurisdiction. Sproul,
a former comptroller, was not ready to reduce the power
of that office. (It was not until about 1960 that the Press
was allowed to mail its own packages, without paying a
premium to the mailing division.) In the same way he rejected Farquhar's proposal for a separate accounting office
at the Press, one that might do title accounting, a standard
procedure in commercial publishing. Instead, there was to
be a bookkeeper, who would act as liaison between the
Press and the University accounting department. Here
again Farquhar asked for something that was not granted
until many years later.

   In the reorganization proposal, publications were divided into three categories: series monographs, works published on special or outside funds, and books. No change
was proposed for the series, although Farquhar did suggest
that some of them be replaced by journals—a suggestion
that went nowhere. Special publications were to be handled on a commission basis. The heart of the proposal, the
provision that began to change the direction of the Press,
had to do with books. Farquhar proposed—and Sproul approved—that books be divided into two classes, those paid

for (like series papers) from the annual Press appropriation, controlled by the Editorial Committee, and those financed by a new revolving fund controlled by the manager. The first group would be totally noncommercial, as in the past. The second group would be published at risk; if chosen well and successfully sold, they would recoup their cost and the fund would revolve.[11]

In order to set up the new account, Farquhar asked that all money received from the sales of both books and series, or at least the first $6,000 each year, be retained by the Press and used for book publishing. Until this time all sales returns had gone into the University general fund, and the Press could spend only its annual appropriation for expenses, thus operating as a service agency and not as a business. Farquhar was asking that the Press become a mixed organization, part service agency and part business. The Editorial Committee voted to join in recommending the changes.[12]

The president, after taking advice from Comptroller Nichols, modified the provision about sales income, allowing only 50 percent of it to go to the revolving fund, now called the General Publications Account or budget. In order to get started in 1933–34, it was agreed in the budget for that year to increase the estimate of sales income from $4,000 to $8,000, with half the latter amount set up as an

11. Farquhar to Sproul, 9 May 1933; Sproul to Farquhar, 6 June and 9 June 1933; Sproul to Nichols, n.d. (May 1933); Nichols to Sproul, 25 May 1933.
12. Minutes, 21 April and 28 April 1933.

advance credit to General Publications. To this account
were to be charged all sales expenses, but for the first year,
in order to get a running start, the sales manager's salary
was paid on the regular appropriated account.

Even in depression dollars, the amount allowed was
skimpy—Calhoun had asked for an endowment of no less
than $200,000—and Farquhar had to look for outside
money. In a letter to Nichols on 24 August 1937 he wrote
that in four years he had brought in $73,000 to assist in
publishing new books, an average of about $18,000 a year,
and he added that the Press was making a double profit on
the outside funds—10 percent or more added to the printing bills plus the margin on sale of the books. If they sold,
he might have added.

In effect the Press and the Editorial Committee now became separate organizations, each with its own funds for
manufacturing new publications. The Committee's funds
were expended directly, mainly on series papers; those of
the Press were invested in inventory and appeared on the
expense accounts only when the books were sold. But in
practice the two methods of financing were soon combined. Under the old regime the Committee had occasionally published books, called separate works, paying out
(rather than investing) the entire manufacturing cost. Under the new scheme of things the manager might judge that
he could recover from sales a part, but not all, of the cost
of a book, and could offer to pay (invest) that part of the

cost out of his risk fund, the General Publications Account. At Farquhar's very first meeting as manager, the Editorial Committee voted to approve a separate work provided that the manager contribute part of the manufacturing cost. And in 1935 a two-volume work, *Fur-Bearing Mammals of California*, was approved by the Committee with an appropriation of $1,000 provided that the rest of the total cost of $8,500 be found elsewhere. President Sproul provided $6,000 from his emergency fund, and General Publications put up $1,500 to be recovered from sales.

So began a method of joint financing that continues to this day. In 1933 the General Publications Account contributed to the cost of a book proposed by the Committee. Now the Press proposes books and may request subventions from the Committee. The effect of a subvention is that the cost of a specialized book is reduced to an amount that may be recovered from the sale of a small edition.

There appears to be nothing basically wrong with the early system, but the accounts were not clearly separated by function and the annual depreciation of the inventory was too small (see below, Chapter 12). But then good management accounting, based on that of commercial publishers, was not common among university presses until sometime in the 1950s or even the 1960s.[13]

---

13. A more detailed account of early Press finances may be found in an unpublished paper by August Frugé in the Press files.

A STATEWIDE PRESS

At about the same time that the Press was undergoing re-organization the University was expanding throughout the state, and the Los Angeles campus, in particular, was moving rapidly toward parity with Berkeley as a great general research institution. Parity in relation to the Press was inevitable but it came in steps. Five UCLA series, broader than the ones in Berkeley, were established and issued their first publications in 1933. There was briefly an Editorial Committee of the southern section of the Academic Senate; in 1934 this was abandoned and two southern members were appointed to the now-statewide Editorial Committee. In 1936 a third southern member was added, to serve with eight northern members.

Meanwhile there were protests that the Press was giving preferential treatment to Berkeley manuscripts,[14] a charge that cannot be verified and may have resulted from the general slowness in editing all manuscripts. In 1935 feelings of discrimination became intense among some members of the UCLA faculty, and there was talk of establishing a separate press. Particularly outspoken was Professor Knight Dunlap, who had come from Johns Hopkins to chair the Department of Psychology and assume editorial direction of the monograph series in that subject. In a series of letters to Sproul and to the provost at UCLA, he expressed the

14. Farquhar to Sproul, 14 October 1933.

opinion that the Press at Berkeley could become a serious threat to publishing at UCLA and advocated the establishment of a new press, without a printing plant, in Los Angeles. The controversy does not show up in the Minutes of the Editorial Committee, which continued on its way of gradual change.[15]

Sproul was concerned but remained firm in his feeling for the oneness of the University in spite of its several campuses. In his correspondence with Farquhar, the latter denied any discrimination, claimed that the trouble stemmed from lack of easy communication, and asked permission to visit the Los Angeles campus more frequently. By 1936 these visits had become regular and Farquhar seems to have gotten along well with the southern members of the Editorial Committee. By 1938 the manager and the UCLA faculty members had combined forces, with the concurrence of the full Committee, to tell Sproul that a Los Angeles office of the Press should be postponed no longer. An assistant there, they said, could coordinate the flow of southern manuscripts—from La Jolla, Riverside, and Santa Barbara as well as from Los Angeles—and eliminate delays. Sproul gave his approval in 1938 but—typically—granted only a half-time assistant.[16] One of the southern

---

15. Dunlap to E. C. Moore (provost, Los Angeles), 11 October 1935; Sproul to Dunlap, 21 October 1935; Dunlap to Sproul, 25 October 1935.
16. Minutes, 7 October and 9 December 1938; correspondence between Sproul and Farquhar re UCLA, 1935–38.

members of the Committee agreed to supervise the office
with the title of assistant manager of the Press. This was a
small start. It was not until the early 1950s, after Farquhar's time, that the first editors were placed in Los Angeles and true editorial parity was approached.

Although there were two southern members of the Editorial Committee in 1934 and three after 1936, there was
no money for travel, and they seldom attended meetings—
perhaps another example of Sproul's slowness to provide
funds to back up his convictions. Finally, in 1938 he
granted $400 for travel, and the participation of UCLA
members became more active. In the same year the Committee held its first meeting on the Los Angeles campus.
Such meetings became an annual or a semi-annual practice, and in 1941 a meeting was held in La Jolla.

It was probably inevitable that the separate monograph
series should have been combined. Faculty members in
Los Angeles became dissatisfied with their broad series—
such as one for all the social sciences and another combining astronomy and mathematics—and asked for new and
more specific series. Unification was discussed several
times in 1939,[17] and in 1940 Sproul wrote, "There is but
one University of California, and some way should be
found, it seems to me, to have the publications of the university reflect that fact." By spring 1941, when the Com-

17. The chief problem was perceived to be the needs of the exchange
program of the two major university libraries. The suggested solution
was to put northern and southern papers in separate volumes in a unified
series.

mittee reported to the Academic Senate, all series had been unified, most of them with parallel boards of editors, north and south.

Also in 1940, and perhaps as a natural consequence of the unification, the imprint was changed to read "University of California Press, Berkeley and Los Angeles."

· PLATES ·

THE HUNDRED NAMES

A SHORT INTRODUCTION TO THE
STUDY OF CHINESE POETRY
WITH ILLUSTRATIVE TRANSLATIONS

BY

HENRY H. HART

[THE TITLE IN IDEOGRAPHS]

*The Chinese call themselves by the term
"pai hsing"— the hundred surnames.*

BERKELEY
UNIVERSITY OF CALIFORNIA PRESS
1933

Farquhar's first book.

RENAISSANCE
GUIDES TO BOOKS

An Inventory and Some Conclusions

BY ARCHER TAYLOR

FELLOW OF THE NEWBERRY LIBRARY

UNIVERSITY OF CALIFORNIA PRESS

BERKELEY AND LOS ANGELES · 1945

Some of Farquhar's designs for books on bibliography and printing, a particular interest of his. *Typologia* was the first book set in University of California Old Style, the typeface designed by Frederic Goudy for the Press.

Ancient Libraries

JAMES WESTFALL THOMPSON

SIDNEY HELLMAN EHRMAN PROFESSOR OF EUROPEAN HISTORY EMERITUS
IN THE UNIVERSITY OF CALIFORNIA

*Qui primus bibliothecam dicando,
ingenia hominum rempublicam fecit.*
—PLINY THE YOUNGER

From the *Codex Amiatinus*

A BOOKCASE AND WRITING MATERIALS

BERKELEY, CALIFORNIA · 1940
UNIVERSITY OF CALIFORNIA PRESS

Typologia

STUDIES IN TYPE DESIGN & TYPE MAKING

WITH COMMENTS ON THE INVENTION OF
TYPOGRAPHY · THE FIRST TYPES
LEGIBILITY AND FINE
PRINTING

FREDERIC W. GOUDY, L.H.D., LITT.D.

BERKELEY AND LOS ANGELES
UNIVERSITY OF CALIFORNIA PRESS
1940

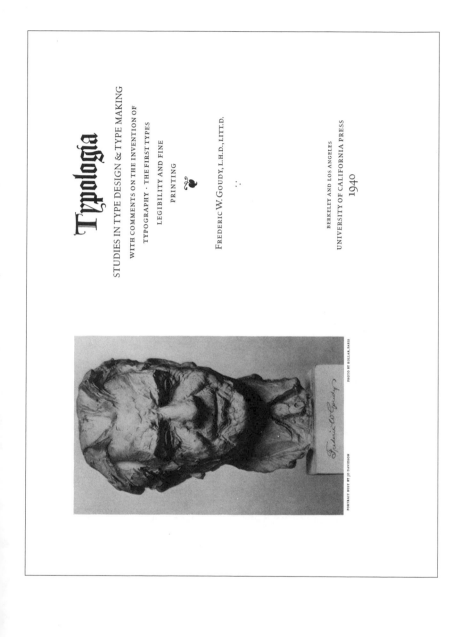

PORTRAIT BUST BY JO DAVIDSON

PHOTO BY KOLLAR, PARIS

The Alphabet
AND ELEMENTS OF LETTERING

REVISED AND ENLARGED
WITH MANY FULL-PAGE PLATES AND OTHER
ILLUSTRATIONS DRAWN & ARRANGED
BY THE AUTHOR

FREDERIC W. GOUDY
L.H.D., LITT.D.

BERKELEY AND LOS ANGELES
UNIVERSITY OF CALIFORNIA PRESS
1952

AVRELIO
AVG · LIB
APHRODISIO
PROC · AVG
A · RATIONIBVS
S · P · Q · L
DEDIC·Q·VARINIO·Q·F
MAEC·LAEVIANO·AED

INSCRIPTION FROM BASE OF STATUE IN A ROMAN PALACE
SET IN 'GOUDY OLD STYLE' CAPITALS

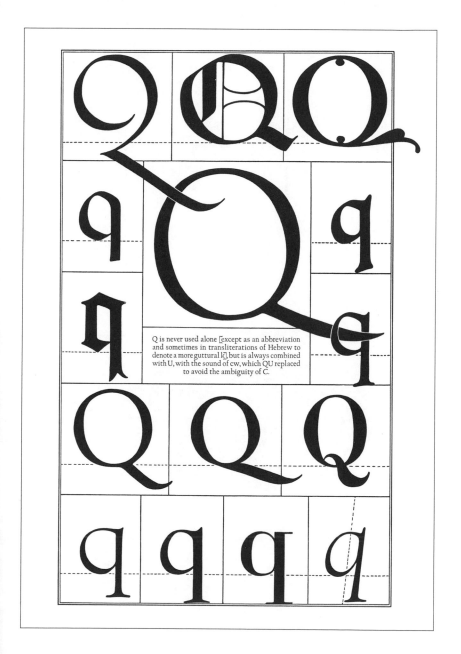

Q is never used alone [except as an abbreviation and sometimes in transliterations of Hebrew to denote a more guttural k], but is always combined with U, with the sound of cw, which QU replaced to avoid the ambiguity of C.

Sir Isaac Newton's

MATHEMATICAL PRINCIPLES

OF NATURAL PHILOSOPHY AND HIS SYSTEM OF THE WORLD

Translated into English by Andrew Motte in 1729.
The translations revised, and supplied with an
historical and explanatory appendix, by

FLORIAN CAJORI

LATE PROFESSOR OF THE HISTORY OF MATHEMATICS EMERITUS
IN THE UNIVERSITY OF CALIFORNIA

SIR ISAAC NEWTON

(See Appendix, Note 1, page 627)

UNIVERSITY OF CALIFORNIA PRESS
BERKELEY, CALIFORNIA
1946

Newton's *Mathematical Principles*, 1946 edition. The book was first published in 1934.

FUR=BEARING MAMMALS OF CALIFORNIA

Their Natural History,
Systematic Status, and Relations to Man

BY

JOSEPH GRINNELL
JOSEPH S. DIXON, AND JEAN M. LINSDALE

❖

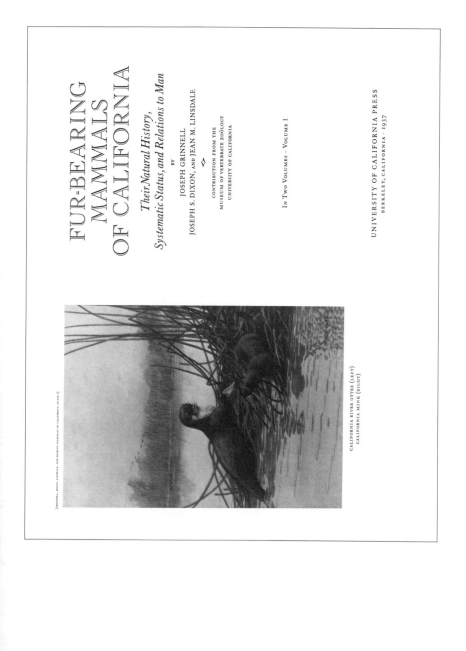

CALIFORNIA RIVER OTTER (LEFT)
CALIFORNIA MINK (RIGHT)

CONTRIBUTION FROM THE
MUSEUM OF VERTEBRATE ZOÖLOGY
UNIVERSITY OF CALIFORNIA

IN TWO VOLUMES · VOLUME I

UNIVERSITY OF CALIFORNIA PRESS
BERKELEY, CALIFORNIA · 1937

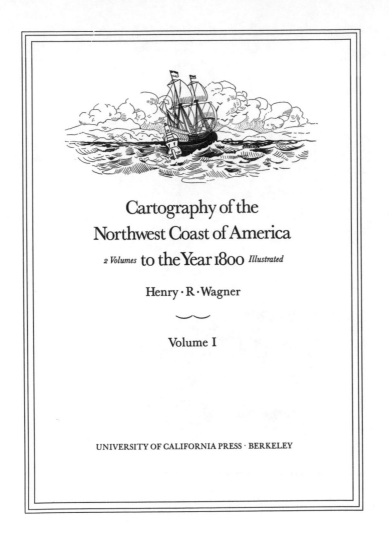

Cartography of the
Northwest Coast of America

2 Volumes to the Year 1800 *Illustrated*

Henry · R · Wagner

Volume I

UNIVERSITY OF CALIFORNIA PRESS · BERKELEY

THE DANCER'S QUEST

Essays on the Aesthetic of the Contemporary Dance

BY ELIZABETH SELDEN

UNIVERSITY OF CALIFORNIA PRESS
BERKELEY · CALIFORNIA · 1935

MARY WIGMAN: "DIE FEIER"

The Dancer's Quest, the first Press book to be chosen by the AIGA show of the Fifty Books of the Year. Designed by Farquhar and Fred E. Ross.

✠ A Historical, Political, and Natural Description of California by Pedro Fages, Soldier of Spain

Newly Translated into English from the Original Spanish by Herbert Ingram Priestley, *Professor of Mexican History in the University of California and Librarian of the Bancroft Library*

University of California Press : Berkeley
Nineteen Hundred Thirty-seven

Historical, Political, and Natural Description of California. Designed by Farquhar and Ross.

Ceremonial Costumes
of the Pueblo Indians

*Their Evolution, Fabrication, and
Significance in the Prayer Drama*

VIRGINIA MORE ROEDIGER

UNIVERSITY OF CALIFORNIA PRESS

BERKELEY AND LOS ANGELES

1941

Ceremonial Costumes of the Pueblo Indians. Designed by Farquhar and
A. R. Tommasini. Reprinted in 1991.

CORONADO'S QUEST

The Discovery of the Southwestern States

BY A. GROVE DAY

Berkeley and Los Angeles · 1940

UNIVERSITY OF CALIFORNIA PRESS

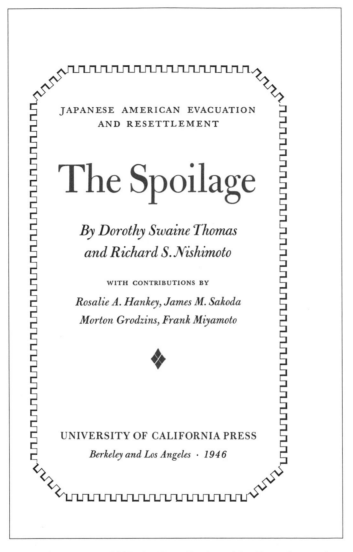

JAPANESE AMERICAN EVACUATION
AND RESETTLEMENT

The Spoilage

*By Dorothy Swaine Thomas
and Richard S. Nishimoto*

WITH CONTRIBUTIONS BY

*Rosalie A. Hankey, James M. Sakoda
Morton Grodzins, Frank Miyamoto*

UNIVERSITY OF CALIFORNIA PRESS

Berkeley and Los Angeles · 1946

Coronado's Quest and *The Spoilage*. Designed by Farquhar and Tommasini.

CÉZANNE'S COMPOSITION

*Analysis of His Form
with Diagrams
and Photographs of His Motifs*

By ERLE LORAN

UNIVERSITY OF CALIFORNIA PRESS

BERKELEY AND LOS ANGELES · 1943

Among the important books published during the war years were *Cézanne's Composition* and *The Netherlands*, both published first in 1943.

The Netherlands

Chapters by Johan Willem Albarda, Adriaan Jacob Barnouw,
Hendrik Nicolaas Boon, Jan O. M. Broek, Paul Bromberg,
Henri Emile Enthoven, David Friedman, Jan Greshoff,
J. Anton de Haas, Philip Hanson Hiss, James H. Huizinga,
Raymond Kennedy, Bartholomew Landheer, Marinus Michiel
Lourens, Raden Moehammad Moesa Soerianatadjoemena,
Joep Nicolas, Hendrik Riemens, Peter H.W. Sitsen, Samuel
van Valkenburg, Amry J. Vandenbosch, Bernard H.M. Vlekke

EDITED BY BARTHOLOMEW LANDHEER

UNIVERSITY OF CALIFORNIA PRESS
BERKELEY AND LOS ANGELES · 1946

THE UNFOLDING OF ARTISTIC ACTIVITY

Its Basis, Processes, and Implications

BY HENRY SCHAEFER-SIMMERN

WITH A FOREWORD BY JOHN DEWEY

UNIVERSITY OF CALIFORNIA PRESS
BERKELEY LOS ANGELES LONDON

The following pages show some of the books published in the postwar years.

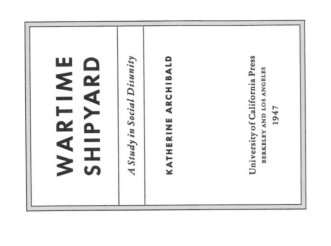

WARTIME SHIPYARD

A Study in Social Disunity

KATHERINE ARCHIBALD

University of California Press
BERKELEY AND LOS ANGELES
1947

DOROTHEA LANGE

California
Place Names

A GEOGRAPHICAL DICTIONARY

Erwin G. Gudde

Local names—whether they belong to provinces, cities, and villages, or are the designations of rivers and mountains—are never mere arbitrary sounds, devoid of meaning. They may always be regarded as records of the past, inviting and rewarding a careful historical interpretation.—Isaac Taylor

UNIVERSITY OF CALIFORNIA PRESS

Berkeley and Los Angeles · 1949

Chronicles of California

GOLD IS THE CORNERSTONE

JOHN WALTON CAUGHEY

With vignettes by W. R. Cameron

UNIVERSITY OF CALIFORNIA PRESS

Berkeley and Los Angeles

1948

Chronicles of California

CALIFORNIA PICTORIAL

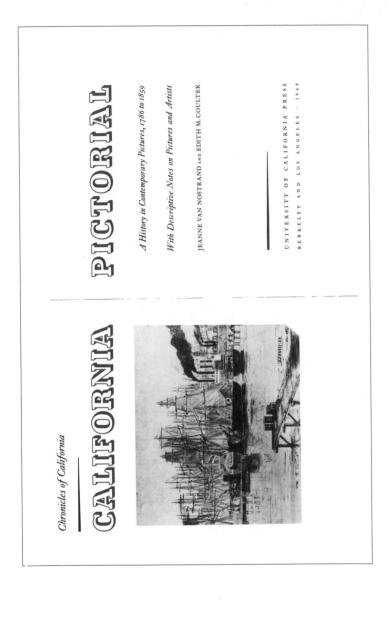

A History in Contemporary Pictures, 1786 to 1859

With Descriptive Notes on Pictures and Artists

JEANNE VAN NOSTRAND AND EDITH M. COULTER

UNIVERSITY OF CALIFORNIA PRESS

BERKELEY AND LOS ANGELES · 1948

CHAPTER 7

PUBLISHING IN THE FARQUHAR ERA

Journals, Series, and Books

During the farquhar years the Press pursued three different publishing programs: scholarly journals, the scientific series, and books. The first of these was the smallest; the series were by far the most numerous; the books, while not many in number and of mixed quality, created a forerunner of the modern Press and when viewed in retrospect may call for more attention than the other two. What follows is a general discussion of the first two and then a consideration of the publishing activities of the Press, with emphasis on the books, in three distinctive periods: the prewar years, the war years, and the postwar period.

Journal publishing did not begin as a thought-out program but started in what seems an accidental way.[1] The first step, indeed, was a backward one—the discontinuance in 1933 of the old *University of California Chronicle*,

---

1. For a fuller treatment of the early journals, see August Frugé, "An Evaluation of Journals Published at the University of California Press" (M.A. thesis, University of California School of Librarianship, 1949).

which had ceased to be useful long before Farquhar's reorganization. In the intervening years there had been proposals for other general periodicals but not, so far as the records show, any move to establish journals in any of the academic disciplines.

Then in August 1935 Farquhar simply announced to the Editorial Committee that the printing department would be printing the *Bulletin of the Seismological Society of America*. The Committee voted to grant the use of the Press imprint, subject to withdrawal at any time. No money was appropriated. The *Bulletin* was not really a Press publication but was simply a printing job, paid for by the society.

Five other journals, handled and financed by the Press, were either taken over or established before 1949. All were proposed by individual faculty members, most of them in Los Angeles, and some represented interests of Farquhar. The Editorial Committee granted the imprint and assumed some kind of editorial control but provided no funds. In one way or another, all were indirectly subsidized by the Press and the printing department.

Pacific Historical Review, formerly issued by another publisher, was taken over in 1938 and published for the Pacific Coast Branch of the American Historical Association. The University became sponsor and provided editorial space and assistance on the Los Angeles campus; Farquhar became business manager.

In March 1941 the California Folklore Society was organized with the purpose of sponsoring a journal, *California Folklore Quarterly*, later renamed *Western Folklore*. President Sproul was asked to be president of the society, while the Press handled all business matters and underwrote the finances. Folklore was an interest of Farquhar, and the journal was edited by faculty friends of his.

In the summer of 1945 Professor Bradford A. Booth of the UCLA English Department started a small journal entitled *The Trollopian*. One issue later the Press imprint was granted and the Press took over publication and financial responsibility. After the scope of the journal had become broader, the name was changed in 1949 to *Nineteenth-Century Fiction*.

The *Hollywood Quarterly*, originally sponsored jointly by the University and the Hollywood Writers' Mobilization, began publication in the fall of 1945, with the Press assuming all financial responsibility. It eventually went through two changes of name and now exists as *Film Quarterly*, entirely owned by the Press.[2]

Romance Philology, the brainchild of Professor Yakov Malkiel of the Spanish Department in Berkeley, was founded in 1947 because of a petition by several members of the faculty. The Press handled all business matters and took sole financial responsibility.

Considering the financial and other difficulties that followed, and to some extent preceded, Farquhar's death, it seems remarkable that all five journals have survived into the 1990s, although some have undergone transformations.

---

2. Its checkered history, political and editorial, has been told in an unpublished article by August Frugé, "Hollywood and Berkeley," 1987.

By the late 1940s, when printing costs had doubled and other costs were rising, the financial burden on the Press was more than could be borne. The printing department, which helped subsidize the journals by reducing the printing bills, came under strong pressure from other University customers who felt that their bills were consequently higher. The costs of editing and distribution were buried in two publishing accounts, administration (appropriated) and General Publications. August Frugé attempted to bring down manufacturing costs by obtaining bids from eastern printers who specialized in journals and produced them more economically. One journal, *Romance Philology*, whose composition had to be done on the monotype, was sent to an eastern printer.

In February 1948 Frugé, then in charge of the program, grew concerned about the loss incurred in the publication of journals. In a statement to the Editorial Committee he wrote, "It is difficult to see how such journals can be published during the next few years unless the University or some other organization is convinced of their value and convinced sufficiently to make an annual appropriation for their support."[3] That spring a subcommittee surveyed scholarly journals published throughout the country in a variety of disciplines and found that no more than one in ten was self-supporting. They also examined figures provided by Frugé. In June the Committee wrote to Sproul in

3. Frugé, "Statement to the Editorial Committee on Publishing Problems," 26 February 1948.

strong support of journals and their value to the University, and asked for an annual subvention of $30,000. Nothing was done about the matter until the Press and the printing department were separated the following year, and it became necessary to give the Press a new financial structure. A journals budget was then set up with University support.

THE SCIENTIFIC SERIES

A reading of the Minutes of the Editorial Committee for the years 1933 to 1949 shows that almost the entire attention of the Committee was focused on problems of the University series: approval of manuscripts, selection of boards of editors, decisions about eligibility, authors' copies, and the like. Items having to do with general publications are few and brief and there is virtually no discussion of book publishing except when general publications were thought to be interfering with the editing of series papers. The Minutes are not a full reflection of the work of the staff, but still it is clear that the Press remained primarily a monograph-issuing organization throughout the period, although the balance shifted somewhat during the war years and again in the late 1940s.

In the sixteen Farquhar years the Committee approved more than nine hundred series manuscripts and less than a third that number of book manuscripts, only some of which were general publications. The average number of series monographs, fifty or sixty a year, is about the same as the average of the old Press before 1933. In the single year of March 1940 to March 1941, there were approved eighty-one monographs whose manuscript pages totaled 12,349, along with fourteen general publications of 2,850 pages. During the war years of 1944 and 1945, when the budget was lowered, approvals of monographs sank to thirty-four and thirty, but after that the number went up once more. In 1948–49, the last Farquhar year, fifty-seven series manuscripts and seventeen general publications were approved for publication.[4]

Series publication was adversely affected first by the Great Depression and then by the war. In the mid 1930s the Committee's budget was reduced by more than 60 percent. Even in those days of low costs, $27,000 would not pay for the manufacture of many monographs. The Committee had to turn away works that might have been published in more prosperous times and urged boards of editors to insist on the utmost condensation of manuscripts. It also began giving preference to faculty manuscripts over the work of graduate students. At times, student work, mostly dissertations, made up nearly half of the series manuscripts.[5]

What the Committee considered a threat seems to have been viewed by Farquhar as a mixed blessing. In his report to President Sproul for the years 1934–36 he wrote, "Possibly the financial stringency was not an unmixed evil, for the Editorial Committee was under the necessity of inten-

4. These figures are taken from the Reports of the Editorial Committee to the Academic Senate.
5. See Minutes, 21 March and 9 May 1941.

sifying its scrutiny in selecting manuscripts to be published, and authors were apparently discouraged from submitting manuscripts except those which unquestionably were contributions to scholarship."

It appears that manager and Committee were not seeing eye to eye. After the budget had gone up to $45,000, as depression gave way to prewar prosperity of a kind, the war itself brought a new stringency. As part of his wartime publishing policy, outlined to the president in early 1943 and discussed with the Committee in February of that year, Farquhar recommended that liberal arts publishing be put off until after the war and that the series budget be cut as a wartime measure. Although the Committee protested vigorously, the appropriation for the year 1943–44 was cut to $20,000, less than the lowest figure of the depression years (see Chapter 9).

The budget remained low for several years, but the Committee then began fighting for substantial increases and made several successful appeals to the president for supplementary funds to clear the docket at fiscal year end. By the last years of the decade the annual appropriation had risen to $75,000. Although Farquhar joined in the requests for larger appropriations and used his General Publications Account to help pay the cost of longer series works that could be bound and sold, it is doubtful that Committee members forgave him for working against their interests. The immediate cause of the attack on him of 1947–48 was editorial slowness but may not have been unrelated to earlier differences.

During this period fourteen new subject series were established, compared to the twenty-three established under Benjamin Ide Wheeler, an average of about one per year for both periods. But whereas Wheeler's series, if they may be called that, included most of the highly successful ones, especially those in anthropology and the life sciences, the later ones were less successful—as measured by continued growth and steady publication. The Committee of that time seems to have believed that all disciplines deserved equal treatment, regardless of their suitability to monograph publication. Of the new series only Linguistics was heavily used, both because the field was, and is, suitable to this type of publication and because much work was being done in recording Indian languages before the last informants were gone.[6]

SERIES EDITING

Farquhar evidently did not care for the work of Emily Wilkie, who had come to the Press in 1908 and had been editor for twelve years. Even before becoming manager he demoted her, much to the displeasure of the faculty members who valued her services, and hired in her place Harold Adams Small. Small, a native of Maine, was schooled in the old New England liberal arts tradition. Not long after graduation from Colby College in 1915 he went to work for

6. For a statement on the value of the series as a whole and for a description of the more successful series, see the essay by Lincoln Constance in Appendix 1.

the *Hartford Times* and then for the *Worcester Telegram*. In 1921 he came west and joined the staff of the *San Francisco Chronicle*, working first as a reporter and then for several years as editor of the book review section. Later he was literary editor of the *Argonaut*, a magazine of general interest. In San Francisco he met Farquhar, with whom he shared a New England background as well as a similarity in education and tastes. The two men were founding members of the Roxburghe Club, a group interested in fine printing and book collecting.

As editor, Small did almost no procurement of book manuscripts, work that was carried out, if at all, by Farquhar himself; series manuscripts, of course, came up through editorial boards and the Editorial Committee. Small was thus the chief copyeditor. When manuscripts were approved by the Committee, they came to him for styling, marking for the printer, and—often enough— revision, light or heavy. It was he who did the detailed work with authors and acted as a sort of production editor, dealing directly with the printing department.

This was responsible work and Small did it with great skill. He was a man of broad culture, without advanced degrees but with much self-education; he must have found the University environment more congenial than the newspaper world. He fitted well into the academic life and could hold his own with scholars in a number of fields, mostly in the humanities and humanistic social sciences, earning the respect and admiration of many. But in spite of his background in newpapers, with their rigid deadlines, Small seems to have had little sense of urgency and not much respect for schedules. He seems also to have been less successful as a supervisor of others than he was as an editor himself. In 1947 he boasted that he had "dealt with over 150,000 manuscript pages, the lion's share of it personally."[7]

Complaints over delays began shortly after Farquhar became manager and continued off and on throughout his years in office. In his correspondence with the president, he admitted that the editorial department was the bottleneck in the production process and attempted to justify the delays by citing his (or Small's) policy of scrupulous care in editing. In 1939, when the depression had lifted and larger budgets allowed the approval of more manuscripts, the editing was eighteen months in arrears, and the Editorial Committee resorted to the only weapon it had: holding up approval of book manuscripts. This was proposed in September. In November Farquhar told the Committee that he was recommending no new General Publications in order to clear the way for series manuscripts, and also that he was asking the president for an additional editorial position. The Committee must not have been convinced because in the following month they held up two of Farquhar's book proposals.[8]

7. Job description (1947) preserved in Press files.
8. Minutes, 29 September 1939, 10 November 1939, 15 December 1939, 19 March 1940.

Farquhar protested. In May of the following year he came to the meeting with a carefully prepared statement in which he openly attacked the Committee for its actions.

> There has recently been discussion in the Editorial Committee and by members of the Committee outside meetings of the program of publishing on the General Publications Account. In this connection I should like to lay before the Committee certain facts and opinions.
>
> It would appear to me that the function of the Editorial Committee with regard to manuscripts is solely one of approval of what shall be published. In an attempt to regulate General Publications, through indirection by refusing approval of manuscripts submitted, the Committee is ultra vires.[9]

Farquhar told Committee members that he "derived his authority from the President and through the President from the Board of Regents." He further informed them that if they were dissatisfied with the management of the Press they should take the matter up with the president. He ended his tirade by stating that he considered it a "usurpation of authority on the part of the Committee to influence policy through its admitted proper function of approving or disapproving a manuscript for publication." Farquhar's statement was blunt, at times even harsh and impolitic, but he shrewdly concluded it with a promise of speedier publication of series papers and with the assurance that he would "assign one-quarter of the editorial

9. Minutes, 3 May 1940.

hours available to the task of preparing General Publications and three-quarters to Scientific Publications."

No discussion is recorded in the Minutes. Two of Farquhar's book manuscripts were approved for publication. Thereafter, with additional help, editorial schedules began to improve. In his report to the president for 1942–44 Farquhar stated that the lag between approval and editing had been reduced to two months. But it seems apparent that the improvement came about because of wartime changes; reduced budgets meant fewer series manuscripts to edit. And many of the wartime books were Japanese and Russian texts, some of them reprints of previously published books, printed by offset and requiring little or no editorial attention. The old editorial problems had not really been solved; they were to burst out again after the war.

BOOKS: THE PREWAR YEARS

It is not easy to characterize Farquhar's new book program or to judge its success without knowing more than can now be known about the conditions under which he worked. But the books themselves—more than one hundred of them in the nine years of 1933–41—do not suggest a concerted effort to plan a publishing list. They are a miscellaneous lot, spread over many subject areas and concentrating on none. Perhaps this is not surprising. Farquhar was interested primarily in printing and book design, matters that must have taken most of his time and energy. Furthermore, he had to take on a number of obligation books from various parts of the University in addition to the scientific separate works that came up to the Editorial Committee in pretty much the way that series monographs came up. Some of these were deemed salable and were financed jointly by the Committee and the Press; others were not.

As for the General Publications themselves—the real new departure and the hope for a program that might interest the educated public—there could not be many of these. The investment fund at the beginning was so ridiculously small that Farquhar had to look for, or at least to welcome, manuscripts that came with outside money, some of them good projects, others relatively undistinguished and unsalable but respectable enough. Beyond that, he seems to have had to choose from what was offered to him by faculty members or by his friends in San Francisco. Any publisher has to take what he can get, of course, but to depend on what comes in "over the transom," as they used to say, is no effective way to build a publishing list. Farquhar, like some other university publishers of the time, seems to have adopted a passive stance in acquiring manuscripts.

It was natural for Farquhar to place some emphasis on books of bibliographical or printing interest. Not only were the topics congenial to him and his bookish friends but they provided appropriate material for the design of small and elegant volumes. Several of these were written

or edited by Archer Taylor, a friend of Farquhar and professor of German, whose chief interests were folklore and
bibliography. Such books continued to come out, one or
two a year, during the 1940s.

Taylor's books included *Printing and Progress* (1941) and
Renaissance Guides to Books (1945); he wrote the introduction
to the *Philobiblon* of Richard de Bury (1948). Other books
were Dean B. Lyman's *The Great Tom Fuller* (1935), James
Westfall Thompson's *Ancient Libraries* (1940), and Francis
P. Farquhar's *Yosemite, the Big Trees, and the High Sierra: A
Selective Bibliography* (1949). These are handsome books—
all but the Farquhar small in format—but without much
intellectual or scholarly importance.

More substantial, or at least larger, were two books by
Frederic W. Goudy, the first books printed in University
of California Old Style, the type designed for the Press by
Goudy: *Typologia* (1940) and *The Alphabet, and Elements of
Lettering* (1942). The first contained Goudy's comments on
the history of printing; the second was a useful handbook.
Both won prizes for design.

There were in the prewar years more than twenty books
on the history, anthropology, and natural history of the
American west. Taken as a whole they constitute the most
impressive book publishing of the period and the closest
that Farquhar ever came to constructing an integrated subject list. It may be noted that in later years the expanded
Press never made a specialty of western history but it did
develop a fine list in natural history.

The natural history list, then and later, may be said to

have grown out of the several series in botany, zoology, entomology, and geology, or at least out of the research programs in those disciplines. Precursors were Joseph Grinnell's *The Game Birds of California* (1918) and *Animal Life in the Yosemite* (1924), two large and impressive volumes sponsored by the Museum of Vertebrate Zoology in Berkeley. In 1937 came *Fur-Bearing Mammals of California*, from the same museum and by the same principal author. The book was handsomely printed in two volumes and is one of the notable works of the period. A useful and financially successful book was *Termites and Termite Control* (1934), edited by Charles Kofoid of the Zoology Department. Notable also were *Marine Fishes of Southern California* (1936) by Percy Barnhart, and Lionel Walford's *Marine Game Fishes of the Pacific Coast* (1937). The latter, a sort of "compleat angler" for fishermen on the west coast, was heavily subsidized with outside money and contained thirty-nine handsome color plates. The *New York Herald-Tribune* called it an "unusually valuable book, important in scientific worth and sheer beauty of publication," and the then–sales manager, William A. Garrett, wrote to Farquhar that "several performances as good as Walford will quickly increase library and dealer interest in our imprint and respect for our list."[10] But these were slow in coming.

The first truly popular book published by the Press was a slim volume entitled *The Redwoods of Coast and Sierra* (1936) by James Clifford Shirley. Profiting from an intense inter-

---

10. Garrett, Sales Manager's Report, April 1937, in Press files.

est in the big trees, it sold more copies during Farquhar's lifetime than any other book he published. Starting more slowly than the Shirley but outlasting and eventually out-selling it was *An Illustrated Manual of Pacific Coast Trees* (1935) by Howard E. McMinn and Evelyn Maino. One is surprised to note that this book, which became a standard manual, had to be subsidized at first. It has been a steady seller for more than fifty years, going through many re-printings. Two small books on the interpretation of land-scape were *The Tetons* (1938) by Fritiof Fryxell, and *Crater Lake* (1941) by Howel Williams, both intended for visitors to the national parks. They were made into elegant small volumes, fine examples of the Farquhar style of book making.

It is not clear whether the books in natural history, many of them subsidized, were seen at the time as a profitable kind of publishing. But in later years, after 1950, the Press seized the opportunity and developed a large list in this area. Most impressive, perhaps, are the many floras, but there are such others as Laurence Klauber's great *Rattle-snakes: Their Habitats, Life Histories, and Influence on Mankind* (1st ed., 1956), several books by Starker Leopold, and the more than fifty volumes in the popular series California Natural History Guides.

In his first years Farquhar brought out books on the his-tory of California and the west, an area in which many of his friends in the Roxburghe Club were collecting. Their number was relatively small, only ten or twelve in eight years, but most of them were handsome and several continue to be sought by collectors—Pedro Fages' *Historical, Political, and Natural Description of California* (1937); William Henry Ellison's *Life and Adventures of George Nidever* (1937); Ruth Murray Underhill's *Singing for Power* (1938); Susanna Bryant Dakin's *A Scotch Paisano* (1939); and A. Grove Day's *Coronado's Quest* (1940). But perhaps the most striking of all Farquhar's books was *Ceremonial Costumes of the Pueblo Indians* (1941) by Virginia More Roediger, a truly splendid volume with forty exquisite color plates reproduced from the author's watercolors. A Yale dissertation in theater research and dramatic criticism—proof that such need not be dull—this work tells the evolution and significance of the dress and prayer drama of the Indians of Arizona and New Mexico. These western books, as well as the Goudy volumes mentioned above, are briefly discussed in the chapter on book design that follows.

Henry R. Wagner's *Cartography of the Northwest Coast of America to the Year 1800* (1937) was an impressive work in a curious and imperfect way. Printed commercially, mediocre as an artifact and clumsily written, the two-volume book included many reprinted and inserted maps and was described in the *Canadian Historical Review* as the most valuable contribution to the historical geography of the northwest coast. The author, a retired mining entrepreneur and noted bibliographer, had the money to gather source materials, the leisure to study them, and the means to subsidize publication. Although he complained about the Press

a few years later, it appears that he got all his money back
from his part of the sales income.[11]

At the end of the prewar period, in his biennial report
to the president for 1940–42, Farquhar wrote, "The Press
has further continued its function of publishing books of
interest to the general public. In selecting manuscripts for
such books, emphasis has been placed upon materials dealing with the Pacific Basin region." This strikes one now as
an exaggeration. With a very few exceptions, his Pacific
books had to do with the western part of North America.
There were the two volumes of Yoshi Saburo Kuno's *Japanese Expansion on the Asiatic Continent* (1937, 1940) and
Amry Vandenbosch's *The Dutch East Indies* (2d ed. rev.,
1941; originally published by Erdmans in 1933), a book
that went through several editions, as well as a few other
works, but hardly enough to be called a specialty. This in
an area that was later to see the distinguished list developed
by Philip E. Lilienthal.

Among the obligation books, the most galling to the Editorial Committee, and perhaps to Farquhar, was the series
of semipopular lectures on international relations given on
the Berkeley and Los Angeles campuses. President Sproul
insisted, over the objections of the Committee, that these
be published. Sometimes he gave money, sometimes not,
and sometimes he demanded that these volumes be given
the imprint without consideration by the Committee.
Thirteen of these little books came out between 1937 and

11. Henry R. Wagner, *Bullion to Books* (Los Angeles, 1942), 322–24.

1945, five of them in 1940. They were virtually unsalable. In later years Sproul gave up this Wheeler-like practice of telling the Committee and Press what to publish.[12]

More congenial obligation books were the Sather lectures, already discussed in Chapter 5. Between 1933 and 1944 half a dozen of these were published. Although none perhaps was equal in distinction to earlier and later books in the series, it is of interest that *Demosthenes* (1938) by Werner Jaeger (later author of the celebrated *Paideia*) was written in Germany in the early Hitler period, delivered in Berkeley during the author's first year of exile, and published in translation on the eve of World War II. Only one other book of note, Ivan Linforth's *Arts of Orpheus* (1941)—not a Sather—was published in this area of future greatness, classical history and literature.

In 1935, when Farquhar brought out the second edition of Henry H. Hart's *The Hundred Names* (1st ed., 1933), Farquhar wrote to Comptroller Nichols, "This is the first book which I selected for publication on the General Publications Account. There is every indication that it will continue to sell well for several years to come."[13] He was right about this little book, which contains 174 translations of Chinese poems, but he seems to have shown little interest in other literary translations. Dorothea Prall Radin's new version of Pushkin's *Eugene Onegin* (1937) got good reviews but soon dropped from sight. And it is surprising to note

12. August Frugé remembers that the Editorial Committee declined a volume of Sproul's own speeches sometime in the late 1950s.
13. Farquhar to Nichols, Report, 15 February 1935, in Press files.

that C. F. MacIntyre's first volume of translations from Rilke (1940) was done as a scientific separate work and not as a general publication. Several years later MacIntyre's other work was used by August Frugé as the springboard for beginning a splendid list of literary translations.

There were a few other notable volumes in miscellaneous fields, such as Newton's *Principia* (1934) in the Motte translation revised by Florian Cajori; Elizabeth Selden's *The Dancer's Quest* (1935); and Joseph LeConte's *'Ware Sherman* (1937). The latter, oddly titled by Editor Small, recounted the author's Civil War experiences in South Carolina and Georgia and was called by Stephen Vincent Benét "the work of a civilized man." Two years later Small published the memoirs of his father, a Yankee soldier, in *The Road to Richmond*.

An examination of the list reveals that, with the exception of western natural history and perhaps western history, the books are scattered through many subject areas and give an accidental look to the list as a whole. Those notable for content rather than merely for appearance amount to a little more than one per year. This is respectable enough, perhaps, in a total production of no more than about a hundred books in nine years, many of them obligatory, but the impression persists that little effort went into planning the list. As university printer, Farquhar had more pressing matters on his mind and, for all his refined literary tastes, he seems to have looked on books primarily as artifacts.

In any event, he appears to have given small attention to publishing as distribution, as making widely public. He appointed as first manager of his new sales department not a salesman but a fine printer, Wilder Bentley. One wonders also why Bentley took the job, unless he thought he might have the chance to design books. He did not, and he lasted only two years.[14]

There was little to sell, of course—only a few new books in addition to a small stock of old ones and the old series monographs, whose market had been taken up by free distribution. But Bentley's successor, William A. Garrett, was a bookseller with the right selling instincts. He did what he could and continually called for books with greater marketing possibilities. In his monthly reports to Farquhar he pointed to what he considered the real cause of his inability to show greater results—haphazard production planning in the printing department. Although he did not criticize the editorial department, it seems likely that neither editors nor printers paid much attention to the seasonal nature of the book market. Garrett could hardly take advantage of the fall and Christmas selling season if the new books were not ready. Garrett expressed frustration at not being able to do more business with book dealers, but he did well with what he had, making use of traveling salesmen who worked on commission, direct mail advertising,

14. Farquhar to Deutsch, 5 May 1933; Farquhar to Nichols, Report, 15 June 1935, in Press files.

and a number of agents on the east coast in addition to one in Japan and Cambridge University Press in Great Britain.[15] When he left to join the Sather Gate Book Shop in 1941, he was replaced by Leura Dorothy Bevis, who took military leave a little over a year later.[16] As fortune would have it, the chief wartime books, the Japanese and Russian textbooks, moved without any great selling effort.

15. Garrett to Farquhar, Sales Manager's Reports, 1936–39, in Press files.
16. Bevis is remembered at the Press for establishing and writing the first issues of the *Pierian Spring*, a newsletter on current publications. August Frugé revived this in 1945 and wrote it for several years until (he says) it began to seem too leisurely for the postwar world.

CHAPTER 8

BOOK DESIGN

The Farquhar Style

I T WAS IN FARQUHAR'S FIRST YEARS that he and the Press gained their greatest distinction in book design and production. And it was then that he and his chief collaborator, Fred E. Ross, created the distinctive design style that persisted until the end of the 1940s and is still admired. After Farquhar's death in 1949 the Press did not attempt to continue his style but moved, with considerable success, to a more eclectic system, using a number of outside designers.

Samuel T. Farquhar, like William Morris, was a designer of books who left the execution to others. And like Morris, he was inspired by the great printers of the past. The principles of design that were to serve him so well at the Press may be gleaned from the short, incisive articles he wrote on fine book making for the *San Francisco Chronicle* in the late 1920s.[1] "The function of a book," he wrote, "is to convey a message from author to reader without friction or impediment and it is the function of the designer to help

---

1. Farquhar's articles first appeared under the title "What's What in the Fine Art of Bookmaking." They were printed in the *San Francisco Chronicle* from 24 April 1927 to 22 July 1928.

the reader grasp the meaning of the text by connotation as well as by printed word. The well-designed book is composed of many subtle points, each of which is intended to lessen the effort of reading." For Farquhar, the many subtle points—discreet use of ornamentation, proper use of printing types, correct proportions of margins and type mass on facing pages, format, binding, and choice of paper—were corollary to the primary principle of legibility. Words and expressions denoting simplicity appeared with frequency in his column, as did discussions of chaste ornamentation. In praise of the two volumes of one particular work he wrote, "There is nothing extraordinary about them, no vulgar ornament, no tricks; they are attractive through plain use of typography and carefully placed type masses. It is books like these that one likes to have about. . . . They are friendly to the hand and have no oddities to twist the eye from reading."

Several articles on the use of Bodoni fonts, the typeface he would select for the United Nations Charter, bear witness to his profound knowledge of printing types and his understanding of their proper use to achieve legibility. On one occasion he castigated a designer for his poor use of this type which, he said, was spread all over the pages, leaving insignificant margins, making the book ugly to look at and difficult to read. He further criticized him for not having taken the trouble to examine books printed by Bodoni himself. A short time later, reviewing another book, he wrote, "The typeface used is Bodoni Book, a pleasant, readable face when properly leaded, as it is here. The size . . . is well proportioned and handy; and it is to be noted that although this is not a generous size for the accommodation of type pages, nevertheless a correct proportion of margins and type masses has been preserved—a matter of much importance, inasmuch as Bodoni type needs more white space to set it off properly than the great number of other types require."

Farquhar considered the matter of format—both the book's proportions and its size—intimately related to its legibility. Criticizing a book for being "nearly too square," he maintained that the classic three-to-five proportion was the only one that should be used, except by an artist who could violate it for some definite purpose. He joined a fellow critic in condemning limited deluxe editions as "unfit for comfortable reading" and described books whose size and shape pleased him, variously, as "handy," "the sort of book that fits the hand," or the kind of book that "satisfies the hand." He felt that a binding should be sturdy enough to be thrown on the floor without falling to pieces, yet attractive enough to entice the reader to pick up the book and turn to the title page, which he said should be "well-balanced, harmonious, and inviting." "The title page," he wrote of a particular volume, "by its simplicity and by the touch of green that it carries, invites a reading of the book." Last but not least Farquhar, an expert on paper, felt that the use of good paper was one of the more important of the "many subtle points" that help the reader grasp the meaning of the text by connotation. Commenting on the books of a printer he greatly admired, he wrote, "The paper is of excellent quality. The choice of good paper, usually adapted harmoniously in weight, color, and finish to the subject matter of the book, is undoubtedly the reason for the success of almost all Rudge books."

Farquhar came to the Press, then, with a deep knowledge of typography and design, acquired through self-study and through his association with Johnck, Seeger, Kennedy and other fine printers in the Bay Area. Inspired by the standards of San Francisco typographers, and by those of university presses on the east coast, his own standards were naturally high. For all his expertise in matters typographical, however, he knew his limitations and recognized the need for master craftsmen to help realize his designs. That he understood this well is evident from yet another article in his column: "Of book designers there are several who are doing exemplary work, but of craftsman book printers there are far too few. When it happens that both have been at work at the same time, a notable book results. When in addition it happens that the text happens to be of real importance, a collector's item is born." The reason that many of Farquhar's books are notable and that some of them are collector's items is the sound judgment he exercised in selecting printers with the talent to assist him in designing books and the ability to execute those designs. This collaboration between the manager and the craftsmen he chose resulted in a number of books that look as though they had been hand-set in a small printery, rather than composed on linotype machines and printed on high-speed presses. Apart from the two books he did with Goudy, Farquhar worked with only two other designers while he was at the Press. They were Fred E. Ross and Amadeo R. Tommasini, both craftsmen of a high order.

Fred Ross, like Farquhar, was a traditionalist with excellent taste. Though he commanded a great deal of respect among fine printers in San Francisco in the 1920s and 1930s, he remained in the shadows of the city's renowned printers of the period. Farquhar had ample opportunity to observe Ross plying his trade when they worked together at Johnck and Seeger. Fully aware of Ross's gifts as a craftsman and perceptive enough to see his potential as a designer, Farquhar made it his business to bring him to Berkeley, appointing him foreman of the composing room immediately after he assumed his duties as superintendent of the printing office.[2] The potential that Farquhar recognized in Ross was fully realized after the Press began publishing books in the early 1930s. The two men worked together harmoniously, producing many beautiful books and winning national awards for a number of them. Unfortunately, their collaboration was all too brief, terminating with Ross's sudden death in 1938. When a small group of colleagues scattered his ashes from the Golden Gate Bridge, they printed and signed a broadside commemorating the simple ceremony. It read, "We, the friends of Fred E. Ross have, on August fourteenth, nineteen hundred thirty-eight, lovingly fulfilled the last request of a man

2. Farquhar to Nichols, Reports, 4 August 1932 and 6 September 1932, in Press files; telephone interview with Albert A. Sperisen, 29 April 1988.

whom we all honored." The ten signatories were all of the San Francisco printing world, among them Harold N. Seeger and Lawton Kennedy.[3] Though Ross was loved and honored by his peers, his memory as a gifted designer and typographer all but disappeared with his ashes.

Well remembered, however, is the man who succeeded Ross as Farquhar's co-designer, Amadeo R. Tommasini. Tommasini came not from a small shop known for its fine books but from Schwabacher-Frey, a printing company in San Francisco respected for the high quality of its stationery and greeting cards. Farquhar chose Tommasini as assistant foreman of the composing room in August 1938 and named him foreman a short time later. He acted as Farquhar's assistant in book design until 1946. That year Farquhar, in declining health, appointed him principal designer with the title Designer and Typographer of the Press, with the stipulation that all of Tommasini's work be submitted to him for final approval.[4] All in all, Farquhar worked less successfully with Tommasini than he had with Ross, and although the general standard of design remained high between 1939 and 1949, it never really equaled the best of the earlier work.

The Fifty Books of the Year Exhibition of the American Institute of Graphic Arts (later known as the AIGA Book Show) was established to set before American typogra-

3. Broadside in the Kemble Collections, California Historical Society, San Francisco.
4. Farquhar to Nichols, 4 August 1938; *Press News*, July 1946, vol. 2, no. 1, p. 1.

phers the year's best examples of bookmaking, models for inspiration and study, examples to raise national standards of design and manufacture. Farquhar had expressed a sympathy for the ideals and purposes of the institute in his articles in the *San Francisco Chronicle* several years before he himself began competing. After his second year as manager of the Press, he had sufficiently ensconsed himself in his new job to begin producing books worthy of national competition. Over the following three years six books, an average of two a year, designed in collaboration with Ross, received the Fifty Books award. Four of these were regular Press books; one, *Quintus Horatius Flaccus* (1938), was printed for Mills College; and another, *Byways in Bookland* (1935), for the Book Arts Club, an organization of students in the School of Librarianship at Berkeley. President Sproul had approved plans for the club, granting Farquhar permission to print and bind the club's books during slack periods.[5]

Perhaps the most striking of the six books is *The Dancer's Quest: Essays on the Aesthetics of the Contemporary Dance* (1935) by Elizabeth Selden. Rather untypically, the text, title page, and cloth cover are embellished with freehand line drawings by the author. The essence of the Farquhar-Ross style may be seen more clearly in two books published in 1937, which might have been chosen among the Fifty Books but were not: *The Life and Adventures of George Nidever* and *A Historical, Political, and Natural Description of Califor-*

5. G. E. Stevens to Nichols, 13 November 1936.

nia by Pedro Fages, Soldier of Spain, both mentioned earlier as titles in California history. The latter, in particular, is an almost perfect exemplification of Farquhar's ideals, small enough to fit the hand, eminently legible, restrained, balanced, enlivened by three lines of red on the title page and two small red ornaments elsewhere.

When three books (published in 1938) took prizes in 1939, Farquhar and Ross set a record for the Press that would not be equaled during the manager's lifetime.[6] In addition to these annual awards, they won five monthly prizes from the institute's Book Clinic or Trade Book Clinic, four of which were first choices.[7] Many of the books that were not prize winners, indeed the majority of those they did together, embodied Farquhar's basic principles. Together they created a striking and recognizable style, a monument to Farquhar's taste and the craftsmanship of Ross.

Farquhar's design work with Tommasini, when looked at closely, appears less successful than his work with Ross. Or at least it had changed, responding less directly to the ideals expressed at the beginning. Whether this came about because the first enthusiasm began to flag or because the two men did not suit each other so well as did the original pair, is hard to say. August Frugé has written that he observed a tension between the flamboyant taste of Tommasini and the classical restraint of Farquhar. Such tension

6. *AIGA Book Show* (American Institute of Graphic Arts) 1935–39.
7. *Publishers' Weekly*, various issues.

may at times work to advantage, but it can also result in a loss of harmony and integrity.[8]

Although a greater number of books was published during Farquhar's last ten or eleven years, comparatively few of them won prizes. There were ten prizes in those years, and two of them were largely the work of Frederic Goudy. Of the designs done jointly by Farquhar and Tommasini— credited in that order—the most successful, perhaps, were *A Scotch Paisano* (1941), which was similar to the earlier books, and in the same year *Ceremonial Costumes of the Pueblo Indians*, possibly the most unusual book ever published by Farquhar. The decorations on the cover, endpapers, title page, and chapter openings go well with the subject and with the author's watercolor paintings, printed from rubber blocks in as many as thirteen solid colors. Here, perhaps, we can see a good example of collaboration by diverse talents. It is also quite possible that the author, Virginia Roediger, had much to do with selection of the ornaments.

Three books were credited the other way around, with Tommasini's name listed first: Monroe Deutsch's *The Letter and the Spirit* (1943), *Charter of the United Nations* (facsimile edition, 1945), and *The Spoilage*, by Dorothy S. Thomas and others (1946). The first is a good example of the old tradition, set in the Goudy type, but the *Charter* may have been selected more for political than for aesthetic reasons. The original, from which the facsimile was made, was re-

8. Frugé, *Design and Printing at the University of California Press* (Berkeley, 1991), 3–4.

markable mostly for the speed with which it was produced—three or four days after final delivery of copy.[9] As
for *The Spoilage*, the title is enclosed in a frame of geometric
type ornaments, best described as a string of bottomless
rectangles, suggesting the flickering border of a neon
sign.[10] It "twists the eye" from the title itself and does little
to "invite a reading of the book." Farquhar was not always
successful in holding back the excesses of his partner's
style, but the results might have been less felicitous without the restraining hand. Left to himself, Tommasini
might have produced books in the fashion of his Tommy's
Thirty, a series of Christmas keepsakes, privately printed
and notable for the flamboyance of their design. For three
years after 1946, when Farquhar stepped aside to let Tommasini act as principal designer, not a single Press book
was chosen for the AIGA Book Show. The next prizes
were won in the early 1950s by Frugé's outside designers.

It is unfortunate then that Tommasini claimed more
than his share of credit. In an oral history taped in 1977 and
held in the California Historical Society in San Francisco,
he stated, "In fact, up to that time, 1948 or 1949, I would

9. In later years Tommasini seems to have taken full credit for both
printing and design. When Farquhar described the operation, first in
Publishers' Weekly (7 and 14 July 1945) and then in a small book entitled
Printing the United Nations Charter (1946), he acknowledged Tommasini's
key role but also gave credit to C. A. Ruebsam of the Government Printing Office and A. W. Halling, foreman of the University bindery. He
did not fail to include himself.
10. Frugé suggests that this was meant to symbolize the stockades of the
Japanese relocation camps. Tommasini was fond of such symbols, he
says.

have three or four books selected in the Fifty Books of the Year. . . . I designed all books at that time." In fact, according to the documents, he never had more than seven or eight prize books in all and never as many as three in one year, the number produced by Farquhar and Ross in 1938. But the myth, self-spread it appears, continued to grow. Tommasini's obituary in the *San Francisco Chronicle* of 29 December 1983 reported, "More than 100 of the books he designed at the university press—including the U.N. Charter—have been selected for the 'Fifty Best Books of the Year' award by American Institute of Graphic Arts."

The myth is perhaps of little importance in itself, but it has persisted in printing and collecting circles, discrediting Farquhar as book designer and almost obliterating the memory of Fred Ross, the earlier collaborator who played a greater role than did Tommasini. The latter deserves considerable credit, if less than he took, but it was Farquhar and Ross who created a memorable design style and produced some of the most handsome books ever published by the Press. The men are gone, the books remain.

After Farquhar's death and the separation of the printing and publishing departments, August Frugé judged that the Farquhar design style could not be successfully carried on without its creator, and he opted for a variety of styles by a number of different designers. The success of this move will be recounted later.

CHAPTER 9

WARTIME PUBLISHING,
1941–1945

IN ITS REPORT to the Academic Senate in March 1942, a few months after Pearl Harbor, the Editorial Committee announced that it had, with the cooperation of the manager, adopted a policy of expediting the publication of "works that will aid the national war effort." In April of the same year Farquhar described a plan to publish a series of pamphlets under the general title "Food in Wartime," and in July he reported that the Navy Department had asked the Press to publish Japanese-language dictionaries and a standard Japanese reader. Thus began the war-related publications that dominated the Press for several years.[1]

Since most of these books were marginal in scholarship and many were simple reprints requiring little editorial scrutiny, the role of the Editorial Committee was diminished, and Farquhar took the opportunity to assert himself, especially in his right to select works to be published as aids to the war effort. Committee members were in no position to interfere, had they wanted to, by arbitrary refusals to grant the imprint, especially since the president approved

1. Minutes, 1 April and 10 July 1942.

of the wartime program and helped to finance it. But Farquhar seems to have gone a little too far when he wrote to the president on 15 February 1943, asking for a statement in support of his own opinion that the Press "cannot justify the publication, to any great extent at least, of the results of scholarship which has no bearing on the present emergency, directly or indirectly." He specifically mentioned "the so-called liberal arts," which along with other non-useful works would go into his third category of priority, after works directly and indirectly related to the war. The priorities, he said, should apply to the Scientific Series as well as to General Publications. Perhaps such a policy might have been more palatable to the faculty if it had been pursued quietly from day to day without being spelled out so bluntly. Farquhar went on to recommend that the budget for scientific publications be drastically cut for the coming year. Again, a quieter approach might have been wiser.

The president was more politic. When Farquhar read his letter to the Committee a few days later, he stated that Sproul had telephoned, making no comment but saying that he would be glad to have a recommendation from the Editorial Committee. The Committee then passed a resolution recognizing the need to grant priority in printing to works dealing with the war effort, but affirming its abiding faith in the value of pure scholarship and its belief that the University should support such scholarship to the limit of its ability. And at the following meeting the chairman of the Committee (Victor Lenzen, a physicist) read his personal letter to the president concerning the publication of liberal arts scholarship during the war. The letter, not quoted in the Minutes, was "opposed to the views expressed by the secretary." In reply the president expressed sympathy, said he would have voted for the Committee's resolution had he been a member, but held out little hope for an unreduced budget.[2] The budget was, in fact, cut from $40,000 to $20,000.

The Minutes, written by Farquhar, say nothing about the discussion, except that it was "full," and give no indication of opinions other than that of Lenzen, but the reader, nearly fifty years later, must wonder about relations between the manager and the Committee and also whether the seeds of future conflict may not have been sowed at that time.

The most important (and the most profitable) publication program relating to the war effort, as Farquhar said in his report to the president for 1942–44, was that of Japanese-language textbooks and dictionaries used by the army and navy. The program was undertaken at the request of Lieutenant-Commander A. E. Hindmarsh, Office of the Chief of Naval Operations, and of Florence Walne, director of the Navy Language School in Boulder, Colorado,[3] with the assurance that the navy would purchase

2. Minutes, 19 February and 23 March 1943.
3. Miss Walne, the daughter of American missionaries in Japan, established the school in Berkeley in 1941 and transferred it to Boulder after the removal of Japanese Americans from the west coast. Because of ill health she returned to Berkeley in 1944 as associate professor of Japanese. She became Farquhar's second wife at the end of that year and died in October 1946.

enough copies to make publication financially feasible. The two dictionaries, *Kenkyusha's New English-Japanese Dictionary on Bilingual Principles* and Chikara Ozaki's *Japanese-English Dictionary of Sea Terms*, had been published originally in Japan and were now licensed to the Press by the United States Navy—expropriation or licensed piracy, justified by the war. Reprinted by offset, the two books were ready in fall 1942. They sold well, each going through several printings. There was also a series of readers, used in language schools not only in this country but also in Canada and Australia. The *Hyōjun Nihongo Tokuhon*, commonly known as the Naganuma Readers, had been prepared in 1932 by Naoe Naganuma for American officers under his tutelage at the American Embassy in Tokyo. In addition to these six readers, the Press issued a number of supplementary books—exercises, conversational drills, and lists of *kanji*—compiled under Miss Walne's direction by Ensho Ashikaga, a Japanese national employed at Boulder. It was easy publishing, with virtually no editorial expense and only a small royalty to Ashikaga on some of the books. Printing was all done by offset in commercial plants.

In the biennial report mentioned above, Farquhar made much of what he called an extraordinary increase in sales, resulting primarily from the language books. Sales in 1943–44 were $81,500, almost twice the figure for two years before, while biennial sales were $155,877, again about twice the amount for the previous two years and more than three times the figure for 1934–36. If all these figures look small today, one needs to remember that they are in wartime—and prewar—dollars and also that the Press had few other books to sell.

The report mentions only one other group of books, the United Nations Series edited by Robert J. Kerner, professor of history at Berkeley. Although most of the nine published volumes came out after the war, the series was dedicated, wrote Kerner in the general editor's foreword to *The Netherlands*, "to the task of mutual understanding among the Allies and to the achievement of successful cooperation in this war and in the coming peace." It had, according to Farquhar, the blessing of the Office of War Information and the State Department. The model was Kerner's own *Czechoslovakia* (1940); each volume had many contributors, who wrote on the historical background and political, economic, social, and cultural aspects of the chosen country. Kerner traveled all over the United States in pursuit of authors and editors, persuading more than two hundred scholars and statesmen to work without compensation. *The Netherlands* was published in 1943 and *Belgium* and *Poland* in 1945; six further volumes came out after the war. Although the books achieved favorable reviews and had a good library sale, they had come by the end of the decade to seem less useful, and the series was abandoned when Kerner resigned the editorship.[4]

A number of other books bore some relation to the war, directly or indirectly. Among these were William Fellner's

4. August Frugé remembers that Kerner demanded a large increase in pay from the University and resigned as general editor when this was not forthcoming.

Treatise on War Inflation (1942) and David R. Brower's edited
volume, *Manual of Ski Mountaineering* (1942), intended for
use by the mountain troops. The Fellner, together with
Carl Landauer's *Theory of National Economic Planning* (1944),
Joe Bain's *Economics of the Pacific Coast Petroleum Industry*
(vol. 1, 1944), and Albert Hirschman's *National Power and
the Structure of Foreign Trade* (1945) were the first books to
be sponsored (and some of them financed) by the Bureau of
Business and Economic Research in Berkeley, a type of
book that would become prominent in the postwar years.

There were a few notable books not related to the war,
seven or eight of them in four years. Most worthy of attention, perhaps, is Erle Loran's *Cézanne's Composition*
(1943), which analyzed the structure of the artist's work
and compared paintings to photographs of the subjects
themselves. August Frugé says that this book was the only
"best seller" at the Press—except for the Japanese textbooks—when he arrived in late 1944. It has been revised
and reprinted many times and is still in demand. The only
other wartime book that finds a steady market today is
Robert K. Spaulding's *How Spanish Grew* (1943), a supplementary text for students of philology.

In 1940 President Sproul wrote to the chairman of the
Editorial Committee, asking advice about a series of books
that might be published to honor the University's seventy-
fifth anniversary in 1943. He had in mind, it seems, something different from the old Semicentennial Publications,
seeking rather books that would have as their principal
theme "service to the state," which might therefore im-

prove relations with the people of California.[5] In the end he got a few works of this kind (symposia on education, science, and California agriculture) and a number of local or specialized books, including a translation of Shakespeare's sonnets into French—handsomely produced but read by whom? The war turned thoughts away from commemorative books and reduced or eliminated any special funds that the president might have intended to provide.

In the end a number of the better books, not originally intended for the occasion, were given the anniversary label, presumably to lend a measure of scholarly and intellectual prestige. These included *Cézanne's Composition*, mentioned above, and a large book entitled *The Citrus Industry* (vol. 1, 1943), edited at the Citrus Experiment Station in Riverside and submitted to the Editorial Committee before the anniversary series was first discussed. All in all, the seventy-fifth anniversary publications hardly bear comparison with those put out twenty-five years before.

But in the University's seventy-fifth year, the Press managed to celebrate its own fiftieth by printing its *Catalogue: University of California Press Publications, 1893–1943*. This volume of 258 pages purports to list everything published in those fifty years, whether then in print or out of print, and indeed it appears to be complete or nearly so, with the series monographs (including, strangely, the Sather Classical Lectures and the Semicentennial Publications) taking

---

5. Minutes, 17 May 1940; 75th Anniversary Publications, circular, n.d., in Press historical files.

up all but eighteen pages of the listings. Unfortunately, there are included among the books a number of things held for distribution but not published by the Press. And the three pages of "Pamphlets, Language Helps, Broadsides, Stencils" are an odd assortment of syllabi and leaflets, some mimeographed and issued by other departments, anything that happened to be on hand, it seems, together with some genuine books, such as the Japanese-language texts. Even with its bibliographic shortcomings, the volume is a valuable historical record. Nothing of the kind has been done since.

In his foreword President Sproul calls the *Catalogue* "an index of the interests and activities of the University of California, a partial record of its accomplishments, and a roster of the distinguished scholars and scientists of its faculties." In a short description of the Press, Farquhar, in agreement with his predecessor, Albert Allen, explains his selection of 1893 as the date of beginning. And it is worth notice, perhaps, that he devotes a paragraph to "distinguished printing" and another to skillful editing—"as nearly free from shortcomings of presentation as is humanly possible"—but has nothing to say about the contents of the books.

CHAPTER 10

THE POSTWAR YEARS, 1946–1949

A Change of Direction

THE POSTWAR BOOK LIST took a new turn, one that ultimately resulted in a University Press of a different kind. The change came from a new vision, that of a man who said of himself that he appreciated fine printing but was not in love with it and who demonstrated his impatience with what he considered overediting, and indeed with the niceties of detailed manuscript editing as opposed to the broader kind of editing as manuscript selection. Authors, he said, should write their own books; quality comes in choosing excellent manuscripts and not in patching up mediocre ones.[1] He may have undervalued the standards of Farquhar and Small, but in so doing and in following his very different vision he brought about what he himself called a metamorphosis of the Press.

Raised in the Pacific Northwest and graduated from Stanford in the middle of the Great Depression, August Frugé took a library degree at Berkeley in 1937. He worked

---

1. August Frugé, "Editing, Production and Survival," *Scholarly Publishing* (Toronto; January 1973): 113–20.

as an order librarian at Berkeley and in the California State Library in Sacramento before deciding that he preferred the other side of the book business, the publishing side. When he asked Farquhar for a job the latter must have been thinking that help would be needed in the postwar years; a few months later he was offered the position of sales manager. But this was not quite what Frugé wanted; he was not a salesman, he thought, and the sales job belonged to Dorothy Bevis when she came back from war service. He offered to do the work until Bevis returned if he could have the title of assistant manager of the Press with the prospect of broader duties. With Sproul's approval, Farquhar agreed, and Frugé came to work in October 1944.[2]

After the war Bevis decided not to return but to move in the opposite direction, into librarianship, and at Frugé's urging, Farquhar appointed a new sales manager, Thompson Webb, Jr., just out of the navy, who arrived in early 1946. Neither Farquhar nor Frugé had thought much about the duties of the new assistant manager. Frugé says that he turned his office over to Webb, moved down the hall, and sat there for a week or two wondering what he was going to do and whether he had talked himself out of a job. But it was plain to be seen that the publishing program was passive, unplanned, unfocused, and inferior to those of the better scholarly presses, as he had begun to learn from Datus Smith of Princeton and others in the Association of American University Presses. So he set to

2. Interviews with August Frugé.

work to change it—a long task that got him into much trouble but eventually led to a fruitful alliance with the Editorial Committee and a different kind of University Press.

He was soon managing the publishing department of the Press, and a little more than a year later, after he had been offered the directorship of the University of North Carolina Press, Farquhar wrote to President Sproul, saying that Frugé's departure would be a calamity: "He has won a place among the faculty and is most highly respected by all those who know him outside the University, including other university presses. . . . He has developed plans and policies and been able to put them into effect so that today the recent growth of the Press in size and prestige is due to his ability as much as to any other reason."[3] Sproul granted the slightly improved title of associate manager and assured Frugé of first consideration as Farquhar's successor—for what that was worth. Frugé made the decision to stay in Berkeley.

The book-publishing program needed coordination and planning. It also needed more and better books to publish. Manuscript selection had always been largely passive—consideration of faculty works that came in with the University series and occasional offers from the outside—and the wartime concentration on language texts meant that there were few genuine scholarly books in the pipeline or in the offing. The United Nations Series, pushed forward by the prodigious efforts of Professor Kerner, produced

3. Farquhar to Sproul, 16 May 1947.

half a dozen new titles by 1950. In the social sciences, the books sponsored by the Bureau of Business and Economic Research continued to come from Los Angeles as well as from Berkeley. Others came from the Institute of Industrial Relations, headed in Berkeley by Clark Kerr, who was to become chancellor of that campus and then president of the University. There were also books from the Haynes Foundation in Los Angeles. Most of these were commissioned books, financed jointly by the agencies and the General Publications Account of the Press. Sales were modest, but for scholarship these books are as impressive as any other part of the immediate postwar list.

A holdover from the prewar list was the second volume of *The Citrus Industry* (1948). And in western history there was Erwin Gudde's *California Place Names* (1949), a large dictionary that had been worked on for a number of years, eventually went through several revised editions, and is still in demand. Under the general editorship of Herbert E. Bolton and John W. Caughey, professors of history at Berkeley and Los Angeles, the Press undertook the Chronicles of California, a series of semipopular books to commemorate the centennial of the great gold rush. But the Press found, as did a number of commercial publishers of similar series, that the public was not much interested. Seven books were issued before the series was abandoned; only one of these, *Land in California* (1948) by W. W. Robinson, was a genuine success.

In one of several efforts to pull itself up by its bootstraps—to build the book list rapidly—the Press looked for possible reprints from its own backlist and also sought appropriate books originally published elsewhere and still viable after being allowed to go out of print. Frugé set Thompson Webb to looking for these, an early part-time attempt at editorial solicitation. Webb, after several months as sales manager, looked more like an editor and had been moved to that department.[4] Two successful books of this kind were Carl P. Russell's *One Hundred Years in Yosemite* (new ed., 1947) and *Up and Down California in 1860–1864: The Journal of William H. Brewer* (2d ed., 1949). The latter is still selling in paperback.

Another "bootstrap" operation, begun hesitantly in these years, was joint publishing with British publishers of scholarly books. One printing of a book, done ordinarily in Britain, was split between the publishers and issued separately in the two countries. It is a quick way, without much editorial or production time, to add to the list. Not many titles came in at first, but the method was used with considerable success in later years to obtain books by some of the world's best scholars.[5]

Frugé himself had an interest in literary translations. He got in touch with C. F. MacIntyre, whose *Fifty Selected Poems* of Rainer Maria Rilke had been a subsidized publication in 1940; the book had been quickly reprinted but

4. He was succeeded as sales manager by Albert J. Biggins, who had come in to work on direct mail and proved to have good sales instincts. Webb moved up quickly; in late 1947 he went to the University of Wisconsin Press as director and spent the rest of his working life there.
5. August Frugé, *Metamorphoses of the University of California Press* (Berkeley, 1986), 21–22.

never followed up. In 1947 Frugé brought out the same translator's version of Baudelaire's *Fleurs du mal*, a second small volume from Rilke, and in 1948 the *Selected Poems* of Paul Verlaine. Although only moderately salable, these bilingual editions added sparkle to the list; after 1956, when the advent of paperback publishing showed that literary works sold well at low prices, a great flowering of the translation list began, one that continues actively to the present time.[6]

An important book relating to wartime experience was *The Spoilage* (1946), the first volume of a large study headed by Dorothy S. Thomas and subtitled *Japanese American Evacuation and Resettlement*. A second volume, *The Salvage*, came later. Two much more popular books relating to the war were *Wartime Shipyard* (1947) by Katherine Archibald, and *Wear it Proudly: Letters of a Japanese American Soldier* (1947) by William S. Tsuchida. Both books were advocated by David Brower, an editor just back from the war himself.[7]

Among books that led to other books was *The Unfolding of Artistic Activity* (1948) by Henry Schaefer-Simmern. Not only did the book do well itself but the author brought in his friend Rudolf Arnheim, who over the years wrote more than half a dozen books for the Press, beginning with *Art and Visual Perception: A Psychology of the Creative Eye*

6. August Frugé, "Translations and Other Poetry" (unpublished manuscript, 1989).
7. Brower worked at the Press until 1953, when he went to the Sierra Club as executive director.

(1954), a classic work that has gone through a number of editions. So began one of the most successful author-publisher relationships in the history of the Press. And in 1949 came the *Proceedings of the Berkeley Symposium on Mathematical Statistics and Probability*, edited by Jerzy Neyman. In the next twenty-five years five other symposia came out of the same statistical laboratory, the last one in six large volumes.

There were a few other notable titles, including Charles Gulick's *Austria from Habsburg to Hitler* (two vols., 1948) and Benjamin Franklin's *Autobiography* and his *Memoirs*, both edited by Max Farrand and published in 1949 in cooperation with the Huntington Library. All in all, the immediate postwar publication lists are not greatly impressive, but they do show a conscious effort to improve and they demonstrate the possibility of future growth in both size and quality.

But if the books were to be published effectively—made known to the public, general or scholarly, that might want them—the whole publishing process had to be rationalized and related to the seasonal nature of the book business, a matter obvious enough to former sales manager Garrett and to successful commercial and scholarly houses but of little importance to the printing shop and the chief editor. In a surviving memorandum of May 1947 to President Sproul,[8] Frugé wrote that his job now included coordinat-

8. At the time of his offer from North Carolina. In the University Archives and also in the Press files.

ing editorial, production, and sales activities; planning seasonal lists; setting edition sizes and prices; making financial arrangements with authors; and working out advance plans for advertising and sales—things never done before for the most part. Much of the work he had to do himself. Thus, he had to be his own production manager since there was no such office in the publishing department; he dealt with the printing department and with the occasional outside printers on cost estimates and on schedules. This meant, to some extent at least, that he had to put himself down between Editor Small and the printers. And since no one was accustomed to schedules and since manufacturing costs in Berkeley were out of line with costs in other parts of the country, there was bound to be trouble.

Trouble first came, as it happened, not with the printing plant but with the Editorial Committee, in relation primarily to the series monographs. Less active during the later war years, the series proliferated with increased postwar appropriations and became once more the dominant form of publication. The tension between the Committee and the Press appeared suddenly at the meeting of 22 November 1947, after the Committee had been requested by the northern section of the Academic Senate to investigate the need for greater speed in the printing of publications. This must have surprised Farquhar, since the Committee's report of the previous spring had stated that editorial work was virtually up to date. Perhaps it was slowing down again with the approval of more manuscripts. It seems likely too that earlier difficulties had festered in the minds of some faculty members.

In any event, the matter quickly blew up into a full-scale attack on the Press, led by B. H. Bronson, the chairman, Edward Meylan, and to some extent by William Matthews, with at least some support from other members. To the complaints about slowness was added the charge of overediting—too much revision in the editorial department. This time Farquhar did not defend himself as he had in 1940 and on other occasions, and he had nothing to say about the need to give preference to administrative bulletins. Perhaps everyone knew that the problem was not in the plant but in the editorial department. There is a question too about Farquhar's declining health and the effect on him of the sudden death of his second wife a few months before. So it was Frugé who stepped in and offered to appoint one member of the editorial staff as an expediter who would set up schedules and try to speed manuscripts through editing and production.[9] Then or at some later point he proposed to complete short papers within six months and longer ones within a year. The expediter would also examine newly submitted manuscripts to see that they were in proper form and would ask the Committee to return to authors or boards those that were not. The

9. Minutes, 22 November 1947 and later. With this meeting the Minutes suddenly become fuller and more detailed than before, reporting on discussion in a way not done earlier, and one wonders who wrote them, although they are signed by Farquhar. Frugé does not remember, but his own Minutes after May 1949 are full in much the same way.

Committee accepted the offer and asked for a monthly progress report.

Not content with making its point about slow and over-zealous editing, the Committee went on to consider the limit of its own authority. Instead of holding up General Publications by refusing to approve them, as it had in the past, the move this time soon became an attempt to take control of them. A subcommittee was appointed to study the Committee's rule Number 1, which spelled out its duties and powers as provided by the regents and the Academic Senate, and to consider also the historical development of Committee and Press. At the meeting of 27 February 1948 the subcommittee reported at great length, and the full Committee revised rule Number 1 in a way that is not entirely clear but appears to claim the power to select as well as to approve General Publications. Rather inconsistently it then voted against asking the president for a special fund to finance outside manuscripts that it might select but that could not pay their own way.

There must have been some tacit understanding that the president was not apt to give the Committee a new risk fund and that it could not tell the manager what to publish on his funds. But meanwhile Frugé was asked to report at each meeting on manuscripts submitted but not accepted as General Publications. This he did for the rest of the academic year, and the Committee went through the motions of formally rejecting them all. It was a rather ludicrous performance, he remembers, and the next fall the new chairman, Theodore McCown, told him to forget the matter.

The Committee's postulated right to select General Publications seems never to have been discussed again. Possible reasons are that Bronson and Meylan went off the Committee, that other members realized the futility of the move, and that the Committee was happy with the new efforts to speed up the handling of series manuscripts. A few months later Farquhar died suddenly, and there were more critical matters to think about.

The expediting of series papers as well as the attempt to schedule and control the cost of new books must have had much to do with the ensuing printing-publishing dispute. Both Frugé and his expediter, David Brower, found themselves caught between Editor Small and Amadeo Tommasini, who handled production in the plant. Frugé first realized at that time, he says, that these two men had long controlled the flow of work in ways that suited them. They were now being pushed to work in new ways. Although Frugé was associate manager and although Farquhar had left him to solve the production problems, he had no genuine authority over the printing plant and very little over the chief editor. Indeed, it seems doubtful that Farquhar himself ever exercised effective control over Small; had he done so the editing problems might have been solved years before. The records show that Farquhar hired additional editors from time to time when he was hard pressed, but there is no indication that he ever interfered with Small's running of his department. Now Frugé found that he had to interfere. It is impossible to know, forty years later, whether he and Brower were diplomatic about it or

whether they bulled ahead as determined people sometimes will. At any rate, they took action.[10]

This was the first time since Farquhar became manager
of the Press that anyone had taken positive steps to schedule and expedite the flow of manuscripts instead of leaving
them on hold until they could conveniently be handled.
What Frugé was trying to do for the books turned out to
be just what the Editorial Committee wanted for the series
monographs. In working to get these changes, he took a
long step toward gaining the confidence of the Committee,
a confidence that was to be crucially important in the years
to come. In May 1949, at the first meeting after the death
of Farquhar, the chairman of the Committee reported that
he had compiled some statistics on the length of time taken
to publish manuscripts and "expressed satisfaction that the
Press had been able to work very closely to the schedules
proposed a year ago."

Meanwhile there was controversy over sending General
Publications to outside printers, particularly to some of
those in the eastern part of the country. The need for this
is made clear in a surviving document that Frugé gave the
Committee in February 1948.[11] It is not the best of his
memos; lacking the usual light touch, it is a long and unre-

---

10. At some point they began using outside editors, something Farquhar had done only occasionally and on general publications that the
Committee would not approve for staff handling. The May 1950 progress report states that ten manuscripts had been handled by outside editors.

11. "Statement to the Editorial Committee on Publishing Problems,"
26 February 1948.

lieved series of complaints. But the problems were real enough when, after the war, printing wages almost doubled as did other elements in the cost of a new book, while retail book prices went up no more than 25 percent. The memorandum quotes a number of commercial publishers who wrote that the "get-out" point had risen from about 2,000 copies to 6,000 or even to 10,000.

University presses were suffering more than others since they could not so easily eliminate marginal books and print larger editions of the more popular ones. And a press in California was hit harder than most since there were no machine-equipped book plants on the west coast and printing wages were even higher than elsewhere. Case binding was a particular problem, a hand operation in western plants and costing about twice as much as in the east and midwest.

For the most part the memorandum carried no recommendations. Frugé wrote that he wanted the Committee to know the reasons for a number of steps being taken in an effort to remain solvent. More care would have to be used in choosing books to be financed on the risk account (General Publications). Fewer and smaller contributions could be made to salable volumes in the series. Corners were being cut in manufacturing, with some books, such as art books, being produced in the old careful way while others had to be done with cheaper materials and a lower grade of presswork. Printing quality would have to vary depending on need—a point that may have led to later criticisms that the Press was tearing down the high standards set by Farquhar. Small, Tommasini, and many of the printers had been accustomed to producing every book, regardless of its intended use, in the same perfectionist fashion.

In addition to seeking in-house economies, the Press was having to obtain bids on book manufacturing and to turn more and more to the eastern and midwestern plants then being used by other university presses. The book market was a national, even an international, one; the Press could not charge higher prices than did other presses merely because of local conditions. Two books, said Frugé, were then being manufactured in Ann Arbor, Michigan, while two or three others had been placed in commercial plants in California.

All this made sense to one who thought as a publisher, who was more concerned with the contents of books than with the book as artifact. But the printers did not see it this way, nor did Harold Small. And commercial firms in California, happy enough to get work themselves, were anything but happy to see other work go outside the state. As well as he could, Farquhar acted as mediator—an impossible task. He could not satisfy both parties because their needs, as time would show, were irreconcilable. The struggle for control, half hidden during the last few years of his life, came out into the open after his death.

CHAPTER 11

THE PRINTING-PUBLISHING DISPUTE AND END OF THE MARRIAGE

It WAS OUT OF THE GREAT printing-publishing dispute of 1949–53 that the modern University of California Press was born. Without the controversy and the consequent freedom from domination by the printing department and the University business office, it is doubtful that a distinguished book-publishing program could ever have been developed. In this country combined printing-publishing operations have rarely been successful and only when the first is controlled by the second and operated primarily for the benefit of the second—an impossible situation in the University of California of the 1950s and hardly feasible anywhere when a plant is expected to produce quickly and economically the administrative work of the university and other miscellaneous printing.[1]

If the two parts of the Press had remained together, with

1. The *Los Angeles Times* of 24 March 1989 reported that the Oxford University Press, approximately five hundred years old, was closing its printing plant because printing losses were threatening the successful publishing operation. Henceforth, all its books would be printed elsewhere, and its great store of typefaces in many alphabets would go into a museum.

publishing decisions being made, at least in part, for the benefit of the printers, it would not have been possible to deal effectively with authors and booksellers, with their concern for prices, royalties, and seasonal sales, or to devote full attention to the growth of a scholarly book list for an international market, with manufacturing treated as only one element in the publishing process.

This is how August Frugé saw it at the time. The historian who accepts the importance of university publishing, and who looks at the Press of the 1940s and the Press of today, will find it hard to disagree. And will find it hard to deny that the modern Press was Frugé's creation. The approach of a printing connoisseur, even a hardheaded one like Farquhar, may bring success in the fine editions world but not in the world of scholarly publishing, especially in a large and complex university. The publisher must be an entrepreneur rather than a connoisseur. His first thought is for authors, and his second for the soliciting editors who bring in authors. And after that for the sales people who can keep the authors happy and provide the Press with needed income.[2]

It seems likely enough that Farquhar saw his own limitations in this regard and that he too had noticed that the Press made a poor showing (except in design prizes) compared to the presses of other great universities—Chicago,

2. August Frugé, *Metamorphoses*. Frugé's attitude is also shown in surviving contemporary documents and confirmed by several interviews. The following account of the dispute itself is based almost entirely on the papers in the Presidents' File in the University Archives.

Harvard, Princeton, Columbia, and Yale, not to mention Oxford and Cambridge. But if he counted on Frugé to supply what was lacking, to develop the publishing side, as he may well have done, he could hardly have foreseen what drastic steps would have to be taken and what this would mean to the plant that he had built up so carefully.

Could the fight have been avoided? Could a first-rate publishing house have been built while catering to the needs of the printers? Could the same result have been attained, a little later perhaps, if Frugé had been less stubborn and more patient? There is no way for the historian to answer such hypothetical questions, but the documents strongly suggest that the printing side had no wish to compromise; control, it seems, was the issue. As for Frugé's impatience, one may observe that it took an entire working life up to retirement to put the Press where he thought it ought to be. "In the duration of one directorship," wrote the critic Hugh Kenner,[3] Frugé turned "a printing plant located within earshot of barking seals into one of the great scholarly publishing houses of the world."[4] Too flamboyantly put, perhaps, but not untrue.

The account of the dispute given by Frugé in his *Metamorphoses* (pp. 9–13) is brief; based on memory, it is personal and sometimes emotional. "That is long ago," he

3. Kenner spent several years on the Editorial Committee while he was on the faculty of the University of California, Santa Barbara. For a witty characterization of the Committee, see his "God, Swahili, Bandicoots, and Euphoria," *Scholarly Publishing* (Toronto; July 1974): 291ff.
4. *California Monthly* (January–February 1977): 14.

writes. "I will not, cannot, describe how bitter was the struggle, how difficult for everyone concerned. A hundred large and small incidents lie buried somewhere in memory and need not be dredged up. . . . No quarter was given." His own bitterness is perhaps understandable. The opposing forces seemed overwhelming—not just the printing department but the vice president for business affairs and all his assistants; the president's chief assistant, George Pettitt; the printing and binding unions; the commercial printers; even his own chief editor—all lined up against him and attacked, as the documents show.[5]

Against these he found one great ally, one that in the long run turned out to carry more weight than the others put together—the University faculty, represented primarily by the Editorial Committee. The old suspicion and tension between the Committee and the Press, always close under the surface during the Farquhar years, seem to have dropped away. As Frugé wrote in *Metamorphoses* (p. 14), "We invited the faculty editorial committee to join the press. Or perhaps we joined them. . . . In some way the two bodies were so maneuvered that they became one body." And as he says, it was not a temporary alliance before a common enemy. The union was permanent, and naturally so since the two parties had only one purpose, the

5. Frugé's account fits the documents well enough but is not always accurate in the details. He writes (p. 11) that the printing department's "volume of business was ten or twelve times greater than ours." The figures show that it was three times greater; it may have seemed like more in his memory.

development of the best possible scholarly publishing program. There was no reason, he said, for a conflict between
the monograph series and the book programs; the press of
a great university should be large enough to encompass
both and, if managed right, the two might reinforce each
other. The fight was not only crucial to the future of the
Press as a publisher; it was also a pitched battle, or series
of battles, in a sort of war of attrition between the faculty
and the University business office—a war that continued
until the end of the Sproul regime.[6]

The story needs to be told as it happened; the detailed
narrative that follows emerges clearly from the many letters, reports, and other documents preserved in the University Archives in the Bancroft Library. The fight was
touched off, of course, by the death of Farquhar in 1949,
although the basis for conflict had been building for two or
three years before then. The first documents concern little
more than the search for a successor, but with disagreement over that and the more important dispute about who
should control the manufacture of books, the conflict increased in intensity. It raged hot and heavy for the next
three or four years before it gradually died down, settled
in fact but officially unsettled until Clark Kerr succeeded
Sproul in 1958. It is an intricate story of bureaucratic in-
fighting, confusion, and indecision.

6. After Clark Kerr's reorganization of the University, the old Berkeley-
oriented business officers gave way to truly statewide officers who accepted the Press as an academic activity and who—says Frugé—were
always helpful.

Candidates for Farquhar's position, in addition to Frugé, included Small, Tommasini, and William J. Young, who had recently come to the University as a manager of official publications (catalogs, bulletins, and directories). The files show, strangely enough, only a few outside applications for Farquhar's job and none, it appears, taken seriously. Even later when some, including Pettitt, sought to find an outsider to put in charge of both the printing and the publishing departments, no likely candidates seem to have come forward. By that time the chaotic conditions at California were, no doubt, well known to the directors of most other university presses, who preferred their own jobs or supported Frugé or both.

A few days after the death of Farquhar in May 1949, Young wrote to Pettitt, recommending a review of the organization of the Press, claiming that miscellaneous printing, such as that of his office, was subsidizing book printing, suggesting that the Press use offset presses, and asking whether printing and publishing should be separated. Some of his points seem well taken. Later he applied for the combined job. Frugé's letter to Sproul about a month and a half later stated the key points of his position: although the printing side of the Press was much larger than the publishing side, "the future is in publishing"; the Press had an intellectual purpose and should aspire over the years "to a rank and reputation comparable to those of the Oxford and Cambridge university presses"; the plant was a service bureau that should produce dignified and attractive printing but not limited editions. His final recommendation was that the president appoint a publisher, himself or another. He wrote as though he expected a decision within a few weeks. Little did he know.

In July the president appointed a Special Committee on the University Press and Printing Office, the first of the series of boards and committees that struggled for years— rather ineffectively—with the problems of the Press.[7] As chairman he chose Joseph A. Brandt, who had been head of university presses at Oklahoma, Princeton, Chicago, as well as president, briefly, of Henry Holt and Company, and who had recently come to the Los Angeles campus to head the new graduate school of journalism. Others were George Pettitt; James H. Corley, vice president for business; and two members of the Editorial Committee, James F. King of Berkeley and William Matthews of Los Angeles.

At its first meeting on 8 August the special committee agreed that the Press should remain united under a publisher, who held the title of director.[8] But there must have been deep differences of opinion, for a little over a week later, after a second meeting, the group recommended that the two departments be separated, with Frugé serving as director of the Press, Young as acting manager of the printing department, and Tommasini as superintendent of the plant. At the end of the first year a committee of review

7. The name seems to imply that the Press and the printing department were thought of as two separate departments. At other times they are called two departments of one press. No attempt will be made here to sort out the confusion of terms.
8. At that time the title of director could be used only by University officers who were members of the Academic Senate.

should report on the success of the plan and make recommendations for the future. The group also recommended a coordinator, but it is not clear from the wording whether he was to deal only with miscellaneous printing or was to consider other matters. One may read between the lines what soon came out in the open, that the basic dispute was over control of the manufacturing work of the publishing program, and hence control of publishing itself. Whether all members understood this at first is not clear.

For one reason or another Sproul delayed, and it was not until 25 November that he took action, approving the separation, or partial separation—two departments of one Press—and making the three recommended appointments. But both Frugé and Young were made acting managers, half-way titles that they worked under for the better part of two years. The president also asked Brandt's committee to continue as a committee of review and to report in a year or less.

More controversial was the president's request that Young report to him as soon as possible "on the more efficient coordination of the publishing and printing departments of the University Press." That the head of one department was asked to report on the work of two departments was bound to bring objections. Both Frugé and the Editorial Committee protested and asked for the same privilege. Both also hammered away on three points: the publishing department alone should be called the University Press; its head should be called director and have Academic Senate membership; and, most important of all, he should have the right to buy printing wherever he could find the most favorable terms. Part of the printing, that is, for it was always agreed that a large share would go to the University plant on its own terms.

This was the make-or-break issue, the one that would be fought bitterly for the next several years. In February 1950 Frugé and the Editorial Committee sent to the president a statement of policy in the purchase of book manufacturing, a document that the president had requested, which had been revised several times in consultation with Young. In its surviving version it appears reasonable enough. Nearly all series monographs and some books would be sent to the plant without competition. Other books, those that had to pay for their own way from sales, would be bid out, with the printing department being given rather more than an even chance—5 percent or 10 percent difference to be waived in addition to the freight cost advantage over eastern firms. In a letter of comment to the president dated 14 February, Young expressed reluctant agreement with the statement as a matter of general policy but said it was based on a false hypothesis, the competence—that is, the incompetence—of the publishing department in planning production. This was only an opening gun. Young's 17 May report to Sproul on printing and publishing is little more than a long attack on the publishing department. Three or four years before his death, said Young, Farquhar had lost control of the Press; after that the printing department operated reasonably well but had to "bear the brunt of the inefficiency and mismanagement of the publishing department. . . . The problems of the publishing department have been completely misrepresented to you. . . . Records have been deliberately altered, University rules completely ignored." After four pages of charges like these, he stated that the problems of the Press would never be solved without "a thorough and complete housecleaning in the organization and management of the publishing program." Since Young was a relative newcomer to the University, one might wonder where he got the information on which to base such charges. A partial answer may be found a few months later in the report of an outside surveyor.

Meanwhile, on a slightly higher plane, the struggle over the control of manufacturing intensified. On 14 April 1950 Vice President Corley wrote to the president saying he had ruled that all book printing jobs were to go to the University plant for the remainder of the fiscal year and suggesting that both parts of the Press be responsible to one administrative officer, presumably himself. Whether he intended to throw down the gauntlet is not clear, but in less than three weeks there were strong protests not only from Frugé but also from John D. Hicks, a respected professor of history, and from the Editorial Committee, after a special meeting attended by past and future chairmen. And even Joseph Brandt, who generally seems to have been a compromiser, reacted with uncharacteristic force. "I can assure you that if one wants to destroy the University of California Press, this is the surest way of doing it."[9] He was

9. Brandt to Sproul, 2 May 1950.

referring to the proposal to put the combined Press under the business office.

The president instructed the purchasing office, a branch of the business office, to release for bids the two book jobs that were being blocked, but the instruction seems to have been interpreted narrowly, with everything else being held up. Frugé, after protesting, noted that the Press wished to bid out only 15 percent or 20 percent of its work. Since all its work amounted to no more than 20 percent of the printing office's volume, the work in dispute came to only about 3 percent of the plant's volume—vital to the publishing program but relatively unimportant to the plant. Clearly the issue was not dollars but control.

Brandt, rather miffed that Corley had also suggested a new committee of review, held three long meetings of the old committee—meetings that must have been notable for disagreement, which succeeded only in recommending continuance of the status quo pending further study. In the meantime the group prepared a complex set of interim rules for the coordination of printing and publishing—that is, for placing book printing inside and outside the plant. More important, the committee suggested an independent outside survey of both operations.

With Sproul's approval Brandt obtained the services of Morris Goldman of J. K. Lasser & Company, New York. Goldman's report of 20 September 1950, prepared while vacationing in California, dealt mostly with the operation of the printing department and considered publishing only as it related to the plant.[10] Plant productivity was low, he said, and costs considerably higher than those of eastern firms. Although the plant might be given time to improve, the publishing department should be allowed to control costs by going outside. A definite separation was recommended, with a coordinator or general manager to watch over both. As for individuals, Frugé was not mentioned; Young was judged capable of being a good manager; Tommasini was called a craftsman who lacked the qualities of a superintendent. Goldman gained the impression, he said, that the cause of friction between the two departments could be attributed to Tommasini's "method of generating problems." This "method" may well have had something to do with Young's attack on Farquhar and the publishing department's past, something he himself could have known little about.

The specifics of Goldman's report might have settled the matter of what should be printed where, but they did not. The conflict went on. At its next meeting in November the president's special committee[11] seems to have spent most of its time discussing personalities, but on 5 January 1951, in its final report, it recommended that the president appoint a manager of the publishing department (no name mentioned), a joint business manager of the two departments—

10. Complete copy in the Presidents' File; partial copy in the Press files.
11. With the two Editorial Committee members now being George R. Stewart of Berkeley and Wayland D. Hand of Los Angeles, replacing King and Matthews, both on sabbatical leave.

proposed by Corley—and a board of governors to coordinate and adjudicate differences. The board, it said, should consist of three members of the Editorial Committee and two administrative officers. As chairman it recommended Arthur E. Hutson, a professor of English in Berkeley.

On 19 April the president appointed the University Press and Printing Department Board: Hutson, Stewart, Brandt, Corley, Pettitt. This was, with one exception, the same group as before, and it was now nearly two years since the death of Farquhar. Nothing was said about a joint business manager. Perhaps the board thought it could soon solve the conflict.

At this point there are gaps in the Presidents' File, or perhaps few papers went into it. The Press files include quite a number of letters from Frugé to Hutson and the board, whose role Frugé seems to have regarded as judicial (and rather ineffectual). The letters have to do with the purchase of paper, Press expense accounts (under attack by Corley and his assistant, James M. Miller), and other matters. A bitter quarrel arose in early 1952, when Young discussed the policies of the publishing department in front of the Graphic Arts Council of California, a group of commercial printers. The group approved a resolution against the expansion of University publishing, and one printer was quoted as saying, "It is a step toward socialization when the U.C. Press goes into the general publishing field."[12] After protests by Frugé and the Editorial Com-

12. *Pacific Printer and Publisher* (February 1952): 17.

mittee, both to the board and to Sproul, Young was hotly defended by the business office and even, with some equivocation, by the president for an action that the Committee called "a violation of ordinary ethics." Throughout the spring angry letters went back and forth about this incident and about a statement by Miller that the University should not do general publishing.[13]

It is hard to believe, especially after Goldman's report, that Hutson's board now repeated the restrictive action taken by Corley alone nearly two years before. In January 1952 Corley wrote to Hutson restating the old story about the harmful effects of sending out printing, saying that the plant might have to lay off employees or operate in the red. On 16 February Hutson informed Sproul of the board's ruling that for the rest of the fiscal year all books would have to be made in the printing department; he himself would adjudicate any difficulties. In response to Frugé's protest, Sproul requested cooperation during an "experimental period"—an experiment to be performed after nearly three years of operation since the death of Farquhar. When asked in a recent interview why a board including three Editorial Committee members went along with such a regressive action, Frugé said that both Hutson and Stewart were "wishy-washy," and Brandt not as strong as he might have been. A personal and unproved opinion, of course, but it is worth noting that the Editorial Committee's protest was approved unanimously by all other mem-

13. Stewart to Sproul, 15 March 1952; Miller to Stewart, 2 April 1952.

bers, with these three recorded as not voting.[14] Without pressure from the rest of the Committee, Hutson and Stewart might have thrown away a victory that was almost in hand. In the following year, when R. L. Usinger and Foster H. Sherwood became chairman and vice chairman, the Committee's actions became more incisive and the faculty's influence rose again.

There is no record to show that the board's action was rescinded, but Hutson, under pressure from the Committee, approved sending three manuscripts out for bids, an act that prompted Miller to write to the president about the likelihood—temporarily deferred by him, he said—that printing employees would have to be laid off, bringing about trouble with the unions and even perhaps with the state legislature.[15] Letters flew back and forth all that month of April. On the eighteenth Hutson attended a meeting, called by Young, with representatives of three unions to discuss "the possible curtailment of publishing activities."[16] Hutson, who by now may have become convinced that books dependent on sales could not be manufactured in the local plant, had given Young a list of promised work for the next twelve months. To Young it was insufficient and he called in the union people to discuss layoffs.

The union attitude was, of course, that "under no cir-

14. Report [of the Editorial Committee] on the University Press, 15 March 1952 (enclosure in Stewart to Sproul, 18 March 1952).
15. Miller to Sproul, 3 April 1952.
16. Hutson to Sproul, 19 April 1952.

cumstances should any printing be done outside the state of California." A Mr. Hogan of the bookbinders' union suggested a subsidy fund to make up the difference between local and eastern costs. Hutson now recommended this to Sproul. So did Pettitt a few days later, and so, on 13 May, did the University Press and Printing Department Board. A week later Frugé wrote to the president, saying that he saw no problem with a temporary subsidy but foresaw serious difficulties with a permanent one. Scheduling as well as cost was a problem. A subsidy would eliminate healthy competition. Comparative estimates could not be had from eastern firms if they got no work. The new move would upset the publishing department after it had made a success of separate operation. "If the printing department has a problem," he added, it should be "attacked directly and in terms of its own organization."[17]

Several weeks later Frugé again wrote to Sproul, listing seven urgent books ready for production. Two of these he had sent to the printing department at a loss of $1,544 which, he said, the president might wish to subsidize; on the other five he asked permission to obtain bids. There is no record of an answer, which may have come by telephone. At the same time the president prepared to request from the regents a "labor-cost-differential subsidy" of $12,500 for the fiscal year 1952–53, named and calculated by Pettitt and recommended by Corley, both thereby admitting that the printing plant could not compete with

17. Frugé to Sproul, 20 May 1952.

eastern prices.[18] On 11 September the proposal was taken
to the regents' Committee on Finance and Business Management, which promptly turned it down.

Meanwhile the University Press and Printing Department Board made one more attempt to put printing and
publishing together again, an idea that now seems—and
might have seemed then, three years after Farquhar's
death—more sentimental than useful.[19] Corley's motives
are understandable, since a single head would have been at
least partly in his power. Pettitt usually went along with
Corley. But one wonders what Hutson and Stewart were
thinking about. Brandt, who was not present at the meeting, had always been unhappy about separation, perhaps
because of his experience at the unified presses of Oklahoma and Princeton. The president was asked to appoint
"a committee from the faculty, with representation from
the business office," to choose a new head.

So once again there was a half-old, half-new committee—the five members of the board plus professors Hand,
Sherwood, and Usinger of the Editorial Committee.[20] In
its report of 13 January 1953 the new committee stated that
it had met three times, consulted with various university
and commercial publishers, considered twenty-three possible candidates, none named, but could agree on no one
demonstrably superior to the two men now at work. It

18. Pettitt to Sproul, 18 July 1952; Corley to Sproul, 18 August 1952.
19. Hutson to Sproul, 13 May 1952.
20. Stewart, no longer on the Editorial Committee, seems to have
dropped out.

therefore recommended that "the press and printing department be operated autonomously." There is no way to know who drafted the report, but Frugé thinks that in its brevity and directness it reads more like Usinger than Hutson, the titular chairman.

Whether it was that short and rather blunt report or the firmness of the three new faculty people would be difficult to discern now, but three and a half years of wrangling now began to subside into a de facto conclusion, although the reverberations continued for a time. There were no more special committees; no further recommendations are recorded. The Editorial Committee, with Usinger now in the chair, quickly told Sproul what it wanted and in brief, clear terms quite different from Stewart's waffling letters: no subordination of the Press to the printing department; separate quarters; separate names; and senate membership for the head of publishing.[21] Quite a few years passed before some of these terms were gained—they all were in the end—but from this time on the Press appears to have operated without serious interference. Miller continued to question expense accounts and travel practices. Corley grumbled from time to time. Young reported in November 1953 that the plant was operating—presumably in the black—with a reduced staff. It is not clear how active Hutson was in his work of mediation—perhaps not very active since in June of the following year he told Pettitt that the two departments had got along reasonably well for the past

21. Usinger to Sproul, 19 February 1953.

year, and he wondered whether the board might be allowed to perish. A year later, about to go on sabbatical, he
resigned his "not very onerous duties" and offered to discuss them with a successor. One seems never to have been
appointed.

So the great—or at least the long—fight seems to have
ended, not with a bang or with a clear statement by Sproul
but with the business office gradually giving up the struggle. What Sproul's thoughts were no one can know, but in
1955 he granted Frugé a month's leave with pay in order to
visit the Press's English agents, Cambridge University
Press, permission that must have implied acceptance of the
publishing status quo. And in 1957, at the request of the
Academic Senate, he went to the regents and obtained for
the head of the publishing department the title of director,
implying senate membership. But he never announced or
made official the separation of the two departments. The
final redefining act did not come until after Clark Kerr took
over the presidency in 1958. Samuel Farquhar had died in
1949.

What can be said about this long and repetitive bureaucratic imbroglio? In particular, what about the man who
allowed it to happen, who sat on the fence while the two
sides savaged each other? A perusal of the innumerable
documents does not reveal whether Sproul was merely in-
decisive or truly of two minds in regard to the faculty,
whose power he respected, and the business office out of
which he himself had come many years before. And he
may have retained some sort of attachment to the marriage

of printing and publishing that he and Farquhar had arranged in 1933.

What of Frugé, who survived the campaign and came out of it with what he wanted? As he himself wrote later, he could never have won the battle by himself.[22] It was the power of faculty opinion, as expressed again and again by the Editorial Committee, that kept the publishing program out of the hands of the business office. But surely it was Frugé who mobilized the Committee, maintaining tirelessly that publishing was not a subsidiary service activity like others under the business office but an academic and intellectual enterprise that belonged with and to the academic side of the University. Some faculty leaders tended to waver, but there were many who saw clearly and stood firmly for what they felt was theirs—King, Hand, Sherwood, Usinger, and others. Senate membership for the director, which they engineered, implied acceptance of that particular director but it was also, and more important, a statement that the Press—even though a part of the administration—should never be divorced from the faculty.

In terms of the Press itself, one may ask what was lost in the winning. The observer, nearly forty years later, may take note that Frugé, in making possible and eventually building the kind of press he wanted, effectively destroyed Farquhar's press. The best of the new books may have equaled in design the best of the old ones, but the impulse behind them was different. What was lost was what Far-

22. *Metamorphoses*, 13–16.

quhar had dreamed and then constructed, a small book manufactury of the highest quality, halfway between a private print shop and a commercial plant, where a few splendid volumes could be put together with perfectionist care by a local staff of skillful printers and an equally skillful editor, Harold Small, who worked closely with Tommasini in the later Farquhar years. It is no wonder, perhaps, that the two of them joined in bitter opposition to Frugé.[23]

The loss was a real one, but there is doubt whether it could have been avoided, even for a time. Frugé was always willing—his letters show—to put some books, the well-financed and noncommercial ones, into the plant without competition. Small and Tommasini could have worked on these, and in fact they did on some. But that was not sufficient. They and the business office seem never to have been willing to compromise. Control was what they wanted.

Although no one could have known it at the time, Farquhar's plant, his kind of plant, would have been doomed in any event by changing technology. For a number of years the plant continued to manufacture some books, along with most serial monographs done by letterpress. But the monographs declined, and letterpress printing disappeared. Today's university plant bears little resemblance to Farquhar's plant of the 1930s and 1940s; now virtually

23. Frugé says that he does not contest this interpretation, but at the time he was intent on building one thing rather than destroying another.

out of the book business, it is an offset job plant producing university catalogs and doing miscellaneous printing. It might have come to this even without the civil war of 1949–53, but that dispute surely hastened and made certain its decline at the same time that it opened the way for the new publishing program.

CHAPTER 12

TRANSFORMING THE PRESS, 1949–1953

In spite of all this contentious activity, Young and Frugé seem to have found time to operate their departments, and if one may judge by the results a few years later, both did good managerial jobs. What follows concerns only one of the two, Frugé, during these three or four years. Fortunately some good documentary evidence has survived in the Press files, with some of it duplicated in the University Archives.

There is, for example, a long series of organizational memoranda that Frugé gave to the staff, beginning in November 1949. But the most important surviving document is his "Report on the University of California Press, July 30, 1952," seventeen pages of specific information. Dated only a few weeks after the president appointed the last of his special committees to choose a head of the combined Press, this report was distributed widely and was surely intended as a campaign document. It must have been an effective one. The file contains letters of commendation from Clark Kerr, by then chancellor of the Berkeley campus; William R. Dennes, dean of the graduate division; Monroe

E. Deutsch, retired provost and vice president; and quite a number of others.

The praise was surely deserved, both for what had been done and for how it was presented. This may be the very best of all Frugé's reports and memoranda. Unlike his rather complaining "Statement to the Editorial Committee on Publishing Problems," of four years before, this report is neither negative nor hesitant. All is upbeat. Positive, confident, and convincing, it is no mere list of hopes and promises but instead is a clear factual statement of accomplishments, written plainly and directly, with no uncertainty and hardly a wasted word. It reads like a model of what a report should be.

He begins with a large claim—"During the past three years the University Press has undergone a transformation"—and then proceeds to prove the claim by demonstrating that all aspects of the work of the Press had been reorganized and made more effective. Stress is laid on scheduling and planning of all work, on editing as a means of procuring better books, and especially on relations with the Editorial Committee and other faculty members. "Committee and Press staff," he writes, "have been working together, become two parts of one organization." Over and over, throughout his long tenure at the Press, he would be saying something like this, worded in one way or another but always with the same sense. It was surely the central plank of his strategy for developing the Press and for operating within the University, and it served him well,

August Frugé. 1950s.

not only in battle with the business office but in the con-
structive work that went on for the next twenty-five years.

It is too easy to tell a story of accomplishments in terms
of the person who took the lead, whereas the actual doing
is always the work of a team or staff, as is stated in the first
main paragraph of the report: "Three years ago we laid
plans to build the best possible professional staff." It goes
on to speak of five major appointments, three of which
went to people with eastern publishing experience, and
also of six major subdivisions of the Press, four of which
did not exist under Farquhar. "Transformation" was not
too strong a word.

Of many effective staff members, the three key people
in this early period, all mentioned in the report, were probably Lucie E. N. Dobbie, John B. Goetz, and Albert J.
Biggins.[1] Farquhar's chief editor, Harold Small, was not
about to cooperate in providing the kind of time schedules
wanted by the Editorial Committee and by Frugé, nor indeed would he help bring about the kind of press the latter
had in mind. So he was moved to an office down the hall,
given some of the more complex manuscripts to edit himself, and asked to prepare style sheets for each of the monograph series. He was allowed to keep his title and salary,
but his authority went to Miss Dobbie, now named executive editor, who supervised the editors, took charge of as-
signments and schedules, and worked with Frugé and oth-

---

1. Documentary evidence on the staff is supplemented by Frugé's recollections, given in several interviews.

ers in the increasing task of manuscript solicitation. She
headed the editorial department until her untimely death
in September 1964.

Frugé lost no time, either, in setting up an editorial office in Los Angeles. By early 1950 he had Sproul's approval
of a new position there, to which he appointed Glenn Gosling, a former trade editor at Henry Holt & Co. in New
York. By the time of his report in mid 1952 a second editor,
James Kubeck, was about to be added to the southern office. Gosling, several years later, was moved to Berkeley as
an assistant to Dobbie, but Kubeck stayed on until retirement, managing copyediting and composition after that
editorial office attained parity with the one in Berkeley.
The quick establishment of the new office must have convinced southern members of the faculty that the new Press
was not to be a Berkeley-oriented organization.

The report recognizes that the key to a more distinguished press lay in obtaining better books to publish; one
may also detect between the lines Frugé's belief, contrary
to that of some press directors, that this work should not
be assigned to one person with an assistant or two. Although the sponsoring editor system was still some years
in the future, an attempt was now made to mobilize all the
available talent, using each person part time: Frugé himself, Dobbie, Gosling, and others of the staff, plus members of the Editorial Committee and other interested faculty people.

Although the report has little to say about individual titles, a look at the books published during these years in-

dicates conclusively that the new active editorial policy was already raising the intellectual quality of the list and was bringing in works that would become steady sellers on the backlist. The fine group of botanical reference books, so prominent later on, seems to have been begun at this time with J. T. Howell's *Marin Flora* (1949), Howard McMinn's *Illustrated Manual of California Shrubs* (1951), and T. H. Kearney's *Arizona Flora* (1951); also in 1951 the Press took over publication of Willis Linn Jepson's famous *Manual of the Flowering Plants of California* (originally 1923).

There were books in other areas of natural history, and in a related field Brower and Frugé brought Fritiof Fryxell to California and asked him to prepare for publication the unfinished popular geologies of Yosemite and Sequoia national parks by the late François Matthes of the U.S. Geological Survey. In western history there were a number of good books, including the first volume (1951) of *The Larkin Papers*, a ten-volume set edited by George P. Hammond of the Bancroft Library.

Another multi-volume set begun at this time was *The Sermons of John Donne* (vol. 1, 1953), edited by George Potter of Berkeley and Evelyn M. Simpson of Oxford. Leon Howard's *Herman Melville* (1951) and Brewster Ghiselin's *The Creative Process* (1952) were two literary volumes that were to make successful paperbacks.

A considerable success arrived with Robert Bruce Inverarity's *Art of the Northwest Coast Indians* (1950), which has gone through many printings and is still being sold more than forty years later. Other art books of note were

Richard Rudolph's *Han Tomb Art of West China* (1951) and Alfred Frankenstein's *After the Hunt* (1953).

It is worth noting that more than half the authors listed above were not connected with the University of California. Also from outside the University (from England) were Charles Boxer, whose *Christian Century in Japan* (1951) was a critical success, and Raymond Spottiswoode, whose *Film and Its Techniques* (1951) was a useful handbook that went through several printings and may be thought of as a forerunner of the present large film list. Three books that later became paperback best-sellers were *Selected Writings of Edward Sapir in Language, Culture, and Personality* (1949), Hans Reichenbach's *Rise of Scientific Philosophy* (1951), and Lesley Byrd Simpson's *Many Mexicos* (1952), all of which are still in print in 1992. The Reichenbach, as noted in Frugé's report, was the first Press book to become the main selection of a national book club, the Book Find Club. The Simpson had been published commercially and allowed to go out of print after a moderate sale. The Press now brought out a new revised edition and had such success over the years that a silver anniversary edition was published in 1966.

As publishing, the books of this short period are certainly more impressive—both for scholarly content and for long-term salability—than any group of titles brought out in earlier years, or even perhaps than all the earlier books put together. And in spite of the quarrel over printing and the criticized use of outside firms, the quality of the manufacturing seems to have been maintained—"as shown by the winning of more printing and design awards than ever before," according to Frugé's report. He judged (above, chapter 11) that it was no longer feasible to maintain a single house style of design, especially in a much larger book list, and he decided to use a number of designers with differing styles, including Tommasini.

With the Press under attack from the printing faction, Frugé deemed it desirable to bring in the best designers available in order to prove that he was not about to pull down the high aesthetic standards of the Farquhar years. His first choice was Ward Ritchie of Los Angeles, who eventually designed about seventy-five books for the Press, of which at least six were chosen among the AIGA's Fifty Books of the Year. Other prizes were quickly won by John B. Goetz, the new production manager, and by Adrian Wilson, who received his first book design commission from the Press and who went on to considerable fame in the graphic arts world. Three books published in the year 1951, designed by these three men, were included among the Fifty Books. Goetz had two more in the following year; and Tommasini, one.[2]

Editorial scheduling was, of course, only the first half of the process of turning manuscripts into finished books or monographs; the other half, dealing with the printing plant and with outside printers, had to be carried on under the stressful conditions already described. While a publishing house with no print shop of its own needs to have as one of its key officers a production manager or production editor

2. See Frugé's *Printing and Design at the University of California Press*.

whose job is to deal with printers and binders, pass in-
structions, handle proofs, control costs and schedules, the
publishing half of a combined printing-publishing organization may depend on its plant to perform this work—at
an apparent saving of money but sometimes at a loss of
publishing control. So it was in Berkeley when Frugé first
began trying to reshape the book program. For a time he
had to be his own production manager; later he turned
some of the work over to the editor who had been his expediter a few years before, David Brower.[3] When relations
with the printing plant became even more difficult in late
1950,[4] Frugé brought in John B. Goetz, who had been
doing free-lance design work for the Press and had experience with commercial publishing firms in New York. It
would be hard to overestimate the contribution of Goetz as
production manager. When Hutson reported to Pettitt in
June 1954 (see Chapter 11) that the two departments had
been getting along reasonably well for the past year, one
may assume that it was Goetz who had made the difference. For the next several years he saw to it that the manufacturing work, in the plant and in outside firms, was
done well and on schedule. Along with great technical
competence, says Frugé, Goetz had ideal personal qualities
for this work, never letting himself get ruffled.

Sales and promotion was the one major division that did

3. In later years Brower won awards for designing and producing the
Sierra Club's exhibit format books.
4. See Morris Goldman's remark in Chapter 11 about Tommasini's
"method of generating problems."

not need basic reorganization, having been run effectively in the last Farquhar years by Albert J. Biggins, an eager salesman who quickly established relations with bookstores and jobbers all over the country. At this time the department was relieved of responsibility for billing and shipping and asked to concentrate on individual sales campaigns for each book. For the fiscal year 1951–52 a sales increase of $24,000 was reported, about 15 percent over the previous year and a considerable amount in 1952 dollars.

For the first time work on periodicals, previously scattered throughout the Press and printing department, was pulled together into a single subdivision under Virginia Bunting. The saving was considerable. After Biggins left the Press in late 1953, Bunting became sales and promotion manager.

With the help of Controller Olaf Lundberg, an officer of the regents and not part of the business office, a new Press accounting office was established to take charge of all stock keeping and order fulfillment, work formerly supervised by the sales department, and a new accounting system was set up, still part of the University system but influenced by the recommendations of J. K. Lasser & Co. to the Association of American University Presses. It is hindsight to point out that this step, although surely an improvement, was only the first of a long series of changes that had to be made before the Press came to have the kind of financial records needed for good management. But the 1951–52 report describes one step that was to have beneficial effects for years to come: the book inventory was sorted, weeded, and given a more realistic (lower) valuation in the accounts, and a new system of annual depreciation was devised. Frugé says that the controller arranged for the University to absorb a one-time write-off of $50,000, while telling him not to let it happen again.[5] The lower inventory values made for better margins on future sales, and the experience taught him, says Frugé, a healthy skepticism about the true value of unsold books.

This report, and the three years' work that lay behind it, may now be seen as the true beginning of the modern University of California Press. For the first time the Press was organized in the way a publishing house needs to be, and the staff had a clear idea of where they planned to go in the coming years. It seems to have been understood by all that the mechanics of editing, producing, and planning were now in place. The next years could be devoted to obtaining more and better books and to publishing them effectively.

5. Some of this is taken from Frugé, "Notes on the Financial History of the University Press."

· PLATES ·

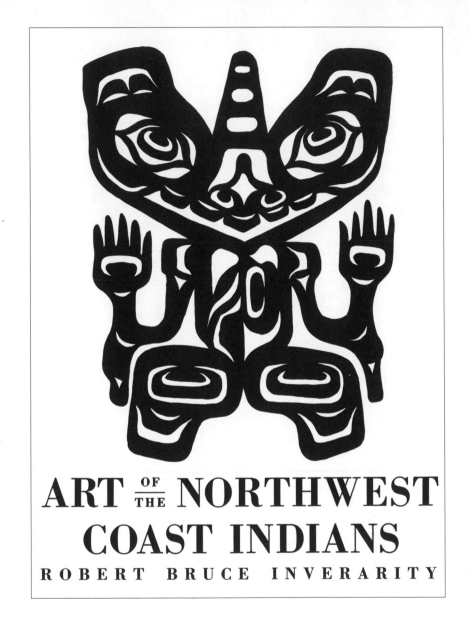

ART ꝏ NORTHWEST COAST INDIANS

ROBERT BRUCE INVERARITY

THE

SERMONS

OF

JOHN DONNE

Edited,
with Introductions
and Critical Apparatus, by
GEORGE R. POTTER
and
EVELYN M. SIMPSON

In Ten Volumes

I.

UNIVERSITY OF CALIFORNIA PRESS
BERKELEY, LOS ANGELES, LONDON

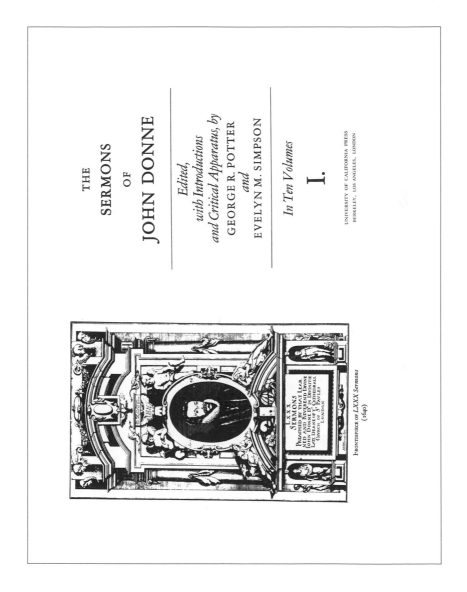

FRONTISPIECE OF *LXXX Sermons*
(1640)

The Christian Century
in Japan
1549-1650

by C. R. Boxer, *Camões Professor of Portuguese, King's College, University of London. Published by the University of California Press, Berkeley and Los Angeles, and the Cambridge University Press, London*

ST. FRANCIS XAVIER, 1506-1552

HANS REICHENBACH

THE RISE OF SCIENTIFIC PHILOSOPHY

UNIVERSITY OF CALIFORNIA PRESS
BERKELEY AND LOS ANGELES · 1951

The Rise of Scientific Philosophy, the first Press book to be the main choice of a national book club.

**✹ CHEROKEE
DANCE
AND DRAMA**

by

Frank G. Speck and Leonard Broom
in Collaboration with Will West Long

University of California Press
Berkeley and Los Angeles
1951

Herman Melville

A Biography   by Leon
              Howard

UNIVERSITY OF CALIFORNIA PRESS
Berkeley & Los Angeles

Three new free-lance designers won prizes in 1951: Ward Ritchie, Adrian
Wilson, and John Goetz. Tommasini was the co-designer with Goetz of *Film
and Its Techniques.*

Film *and Its Techniques*

RAYMOND SPOTTISWOODE

illustrations by Jean-Paul Ladouceur

Berkeley and Los Angeles 1951

UNIVERSITY OF CALIFORNIA PRESS

CHAPTER 13

EPILOGUE

The Press in Later Years

T HIS IS NOT THE PLACE for a history of the Press after about 1953, when its character was redefined and its future direction set, but it may be appropriate to sketch briefly how it grew. When Clark Kerr became president of the University in 1958, he made final and complete the separation of printing and publishing departments, giving the latter sole use of the name University of California Press. In 1961, after a survey by Cresap, McCormick, and Paget, he placed the Press under the academic vice president, statewide (then Harry R. Wellman), and set up a Board of Control, consisting of three administrative officers and two members of the Editorial Committee, to work with the director on financial and managerial matters. From the beginning, says Frugé, the system worked well. The several new business vice presidents, who served on the board, were always helpful. There was no confusion of roles with the Editorial Committee.[1]

In 1962 the Press moved out of Farquhar's printing building and took up new quarters in the University Ex-

1. *Metamorphoses*, 12.

tension building, a few blocks away. There it remained until 1983, when it purchased its own large building on Berkeley Way. By that time Frugé had retired and been succeeded by James H. Clark, who came to the Press from Harper & Row in early 1977.

In the meantime, with the help of both the Board of Control and the Editorial Committee, the Press grew rapidly until in the late 1970s it was publishing about 200 books a year in cloth and paper; the number has since increased to 180 in cloth and about 100 in paper. From the beginning Frugé recognized that "growth is not a good in itself." To do an effective publishing job in a huge university, with several campuses and many graduate programs, the Press would have to publish in many subject areas and become one of the largest in the country. Such it became.[2]

In the 1960s the Press set up a small New York office to handle publicity and deal with reviewers and book clubs. And sometime later a selling office was established in London, which set its own British publication dates. The imprint became "Berkeley, Los Angeles, and London." Oxford has subsequently replaced London.

Throughout the 1950s and much of the 1960s the serial monographs remained the most numerous form of publication. They and the books were managed as two parallel programs. Gradually the series declined, largely because of changes in University research programs. The anthropologists ran out of Indians, says Frugé, half seriously.

2. *Metamorphoses*, 18.

The biologists never ran out of plants and animals, but fewer of them chose to do taxonomic studies of the kind that once had dominated the great series in those fields. More than eighty monographs were brought out in some years in the 1950s; today there are about a dozen a year.[3]

A key to the orderly growth of the book program was the sponsoring editor system, whereby a staff of specialized editors in both Berkeley and Los Angeles were charged with seeking out and bringing in manuscripts and then following them through the publishing process. Each editor had charge of his or her own list of books within the larger list.

In 1956 the Press became one of the first university publishers to start a quality paperback list, in part to counteract its reputation as a publisher of monographs. There were only five titles the first year, but that small beginning has grown almost twenty-fold, and paperbacks now account for about half the sales volume.

In building the larger list the Press became known for its success in a number of subjects and areas. The most notable perhaps was the Asian list, developed by Philip E. Lilienthal.[4] Other specialties were in classical studies, built around the Sather lectures;[5] natural history, including a series of more than fifty California Natural History Guides;

---

3. See Appendix 1.
4. *Metamorphoses*, 22–23. The Press has recently put together an endowment to publish further Asian books in honor of Lilienthal's work.
5. See August Frugé, "Lectures into Books," *Scholarly Publishing* (Toronto; January 1981): 158–66.

European history; art history, including a large group of impressive volumes under the general editorship, until recently, of Walter Horn;[6] film studies, a natural complement to the journal *Film Quarterly*; Latin American studies; African studies; literary translations, a list begun by Frugé in the 1940s and carried on by others. In recent years some fields, such as Latin American and African studies, have declined, while others, notably music, have become important.

There were a number of large undertakings in addition to the Donne and Larkin mentioned above. The California edition of the works of John Dryden, edited at UCLA, was begun in the 1960s and is still being carried on. The works of Mark Twain, both published and previously unpublished, which have been edited at the Bancroft Library, will be appearing for years to come. And perhaps the most important of all the "imported" books was the first complete edition of *The Diary of Samuel Pepys*, published from 1970 to 1983 in eleven volumes in collaboration with G. Bell & Sons of London.[7] These are only some of the larger examples.

The University of California Press, unlike the presses at some other universities, was not originally planned as a publishing house. It began as an agency at the service of local scholars, printing their monographs for use in ex-

---

6. See James H. Clark, *Publishing "The Plan of St. Gall,"* (Berkeley, 1983).
7. Frugé has an unpublished paper on the complexities of this project, "Samuel Pepys and His Diary."

change distribution by the University library. It went on in that form for about forty years. It was then grafted onto and dominated by a much larger printing plant, and its few books, with some exceptions, were more notable physically than for their content. Then in the early 1950s, after a traumatic separation from the printing plant, the Press became at last a scholarly publishing house in the Oxford and Cambridge tradition. The latter two presses are each about five hundred years old. California, by comparison, is a newcomer. From rather modest beginnings in the 1950s, it has grown into one of the great scholarly presses of the world.

The Scientific Series

Lincoln Constance

One of the great success stories of the University of California Press is the unparalleled strength it has developed in the natural sciences, especially in the biological and earth sciences—botany, zoology, entomology, geology, paleontology, geography—and perhaps most important, anthropology, by definition humanistic. These fields dominate in the thousands and thousands of words devoted to the natural world in the monographic studies and hard-cover and paperback volumes issued by the Press during the past century. Certainly no other American university has so long sustained such a rich output in so many areas by so many authors, all financed from a common source and monitored for quality by a single University-wide faculty Editorial Committee. Among those of their authors who are no longer living, Ernest B. Babcock, Nathaniel L. Gardner, Joseph Grinnell, Robert F. Heizer, Willis L. Jepson, Charles A. Kofoid, Alfred L. Kroeber, Andrew C. Lawson, George D. Louderback, Robert H. Lowie, John C. Merriam, Alden H. Miller, William E. Ritter, Carl O. Sauer, William A. Setchell, R. A. Stirton, and Robert L.

Usinger are all names to be reckoned with in their respective disciplines and frequently beyond.

SERIES MONOGRAPHS

Although various forms of publication, from journal articles to bound volumes, were used, it is the so-called Scientific Series that until recently served as the principal vehicle for disseminating information on natural history. Indeed, series publications, largely an exchange program, made up the great bulk of the Press's output during its first sixty or seventy years. It was not until the 1960s that production of "separate works" equaled the output of paperbound series monographs. Thus, it is appropriate that we devote attention to the "print-and-exchange" mode of publishing that was for so long the paramount work of the Press.

These monograph series afforded faculty and some advanced students opportunities for publication perhaps unparalleled in American universities. Although it frequently is difficult to distinguish elements of the Scientific Series from bulletins, lecture series, annual volumes, periodicals, and occasional publications of one sort or another, Muto (1976) has estimated that during its first four decades the Press issued some two thousand series publications in more than thirty subject areas, which represented the work of some seven hundred authors (p. 51). The length and scope of individual numbers varies widely. They range from two-page items by Jacques Loeb and his associates on fertilization of the sea urchin to a five-hundred-page account of eighteenth-century Texas by historian Herbert E. Bolton. Fewer than half of some eight hundred items published in the first twenty-five years of the series' existence exceeded twenty pages in length, although more than 10 percent attained a respectable monographic stature of more than a hundred pages. Later, as publication costs mounted, it was generally agreed that the series should be reserved primarily for papers too long for journals and more particularly for those requiring ample illustrative materials such as photographs, line drawings, tables, charts, and maps. A cumulative total of 1,000 plates was reached in the Geology Series by volume 23 (1935), in the Botany Series by volume 19 (1941), and in the Zoology Series by volume 41 (1936). However, volumes 34 and 35 of the last could boast a combined total of 878 figures.

Because the several series were created and long maintained essentially as organs of the individual Berkeley departments, they were the object of great pride and continuing effort to sustain and even improve their quality. Fortunate indeed was the graduate student who was invited to submit a manuscript—often a revised thesis—for publication in a series! A single substantial monograph could introduce him to the major figures in his professional field and provide him with a distinct advantage in competition for a position in the days before personal interviews and presentation before a departmental seminar became routine.

EARLY DAYS

From its very beginning, the University was acutely conscious of its isolation from the scholarly centers of the eastern United States and Europe, and was determined to achieve wide recognition by every legitimate means. One obvious approach was to print and disseminate the scholarly writings of its faculty. In 1893, during the presidency of Martin Kellogg, the Regents appropriated $1,000 for printing monographs written by University scholars, to be distributed by library exchange, and Kellogg appointed a Committee on Publications to choose manuscripts and oversee their production.

The "print-and-exchange" method of publication derived from the continental research universities and was used by some in this country, including Johns Hopkins. Domestic models were to be found in the publications of the Bureau of American Ethnology and in various "contributions" from the Smithsonian Institutions and other museums and academies. This system was also congenial to Benjamin Ide Wheeler, who succeeded Kellogg in 1899. During his twenty years as president, he discouraged the publication and sale of books but approved the creation of some twenty-one monographic series. Frugé (1986) has observed that "nearly all the great series, the prolific ones, the ones that made the reputation of the early press, had their start under Wheeler. The two chief exceptions are Geological Sciences, first-born child in 1893, and Ibero-Americana, a latecomer in 1932" (p. 4).

As Muto (1976) commented, "Among the more important series which had come into being by 1919 were those that drew on the vast wealth of the relatively untapped scientific, anthropological, and historical resources of the west and southwest. It was principally through its publications in botany, entomology, geology, and zoology, in anthropology and in history that the University came to the attention of professional scholars all over the world" (p. 48).

INFLUENCE OF THE LIBRARY

A very important factor in the establishment of monographic series was the insistent plea of Librarian Joseph Rowell for the generation of publications that could be used in a system of exchange to develop a major research library. Rowell was early given full authority to distribute and exchange publications, although he had little of substance to exchange until the first two series numbers appeared in 1893. These were *The Geology of Carmelo Bay* by the distinguished geologist and then–Associate Professor Andrew C. Lawson, and *Notes on the Development of a Child* by Milicent W. Shinn, a graduate student who later became the first woman to receive a doctorate from the fledgling University.

Responsibility for publication exchange was relinquished by Rowell to Albert Allen when the latter became manager of the Press in 1905. The Editorial Committee, successor to the Committee on Publications, was officially in charge, but Allen administered the program as secretary

to the Committee, sending out the publications and keeping the records, while the library accepted whatever was
received in return. This divided responsibility led to so
many problems that the Editorial Committee repeatedly
urged President Wheeler to transfer the entire exchange
program to the library, an action he finally took in 1914. At
that point, the library was receiving some 2,800 serials and
a substantial number of other printed items in exchange.
The Exchange Division of the library's accessions department managed exchanges until the Division of Serials and
Exchange was created in 1929.

A survey of all University of California libraries in 1972
yielded an estimate of nearly a third of a million dollars for
the value of materials received in exchange. The chairman
of the Berkeley Library Committee wrote in 1975: "The
value of the Scientific Series to the Berkeley Library can
hardly be exaggerated. At an actual cost of approximately
$28,000, our Library acquired, in exchange for volumes in
the Scientific Series, materials valued at around $260,000.
Beyond this the works acquired could in many cases have
been obtained in no other way, since they are often not
available through other channels. Accordingly the Berkeley Library Committee strongly supports the maintenance
of the Scientific Series; and we view with considerable
alarm the recent shrinkage of the Series which threatens
the continuation of very considerable benefits to the Library" (W. J. Bouswma to L. Constance, 17 December
1975).

The fact that the library was the chief beneficiary of dissemination of the series and that its substantial gains did not show up on the ledgers of the Press, did little to endear the "print-and-exchange" process to members of its staff or the Editorial Committee.

EDITORIAL MANAGEMENT
OF THE SERIES

The series were originally to all intents and purposes the property of the individual Berkeley departments, the departmental chairman serving as editor. As the burdens of editorship grew, chairmen began to share this responsibility with a small group of trusted colleagues. By 1908 boards of editors came into being, their members being appointed annually by the Editorial Committee, which now had jurisdiction over the series.

With the inauguration of Robert Gordon Sproul as president in 1930, the University gradually entered the phase of a multi-campus institution, and the facilities of the Press were cautiously made available to the newer campuses. Perhaps the first step was the addition of members of the UCLA faculty to the Editorial Committee, and the opening of series to a more widely dispersed faculty. By 1933, there were thirty-three series in operation, ten of them established since the end of the Wheeler regime. Several new series were originated for Los Angeles, but these were all discontinued in 1940 and absorbed into single, University-wide series.

The Editorial Committee concluded in 1959 that it was no longer feasible to cope with the rapidly increasing number of editorial boards—which now exceeded one hundred—on the new and expanding campuses. Hence it established as a substitute a system of statewide panels for each of the active series. Members of the panels were expected to review and recommend on individual manuscripts, not to meet and discuss them. The Committee reserved final approval to itself. A decade later, however, it decided that the panels did not consistently evoke the kind of critical appraisal that had characterized the old editorial boards, and it moved to phase out the panels in favor of internal and external reviews routinely arranged for by Press staff members.

A special subcommittee proposed in 1975 a mechanism modeled after one that had worked particularly well for the series in entomology, which had just been put into effect for the series in geology. Each active series was to have an advisory board of three to five members drawn statewide from academic departments whose disciplinary concerns were most related to each individual series. The Editorial Committee would choose from its own current or past members a small series subcommittee to supervise these advisory boards and mediate between them and the Editorial Committee. Such a series subcommittee was appointed later the same year.

HIGH TIDE

The series form of publication was particularly effective in meeting the needs of those branches of science concerned with acquisition and exposition of extensive data about the natural world and the native races of California. Frugé (1976) defined the most successful ones as "the kind of monographic studies that museums and academies and scientific societies produce: close research on narrow topics, largely in scientific and technical areas. No one has ever counted them; there must be close to four thousand items, issued under the generic title, University of California Publications. Some of these have proved to be of prime significance. Others, more humble, have provided basic material for larger enterprises" (p. 124). In addition to the series in natural history and anthropology, there were active series, both in the early days and later, in historical and humanistic studies of various kinds. Only two of these have survived, one of these in changed form. Linguistics, initiated in 1942, however, still flourishes.

Perhaps a brief sketch of some of the more active, prestigious, or popular series may be the best device for revealing their character, since each series developed an individuality of its own, and even that personality tended to change over time.

Anthropology   Perhaps no area of research has made better and more consistent use of the series mode of publication than anthropology. This began as the distinguished American Archaeology and Ethnology (A. A. & E.) Series in 1903–4. The first volume was devoted to a treatment by P. E. Goddard of the life, culture, and texts of the Hupa Indians of northwestern California. Alfred Kroeber presented four articles in volume 2 on the culture and language of Californian Indians. Indeed, the first twenty volumes were dominated by Kroeber and concerned almost exclusively with "native" Californians. Volume 20, marking the twentieth anniversary of the Department and Museum of Anthropology, is appropriately dedicated to its Good Angel, Phoebe Apperson Hearst, deceased the previous year.

The scope of this series expanded in the 1920s to accommodate Kroeber's newly found interest in Peruvian pottery, but the language and culture of native West Americans remained paramount well into the 1940s. Kroeber's *Cultural and Natural Areas of Native North America*, volume 38 (1939), which was issued in hard covers, represents a kind of culmination. Theodora Kroeber's *Ishi in Two Worlds*, a best-selling biography of the last "wild" California Indian, derives heavily from data published in the series.

Anthropological Records, begun in 1937–39, boasted a larger page size and a double-column format and was printed by offset from typewritten copy. It was an especially useful adjunct to the earlier series to accommodate field notes and raw data. Its flexibility and low cost made it an appropriate instrument for publishing illustrative material, as in the case of E. W. Gifford's *Archaeological Excavations in Fiji*, which included 288 pages, 18 plates, 4 figures, 7 diagrams, and 3 maps, or G. W. Brainerd's study of archaeological ceramics of Yucatan, which comprises 378 pages, 109 figures, 24 maps, 24 charts, and 3 plates. The subjects of this series had much in common with the earlier one. Robert Heizer inherited and expanded the field of West American Indians, John Rowe further developed Peruvian archaeology, and Gifford turned at least part of his attention toward the Pacific Basin.

A. A. & E. was superseded in 1964 by Publications in Anthropology, which was from the beginning provided with advisory editors split fairly evenly north and south. An Editorial Committee subcommittee a few years ago studied the advisability of combining Anthropological Records with the renamed series. However, the continuation and continued separation as two series was strongly defended by the University's anthropologists and the two series exist in this form today, but they are no longer heavily used.

Geological Sciences   The first-established of the truly "scientific" series made no mystery of its status or management. Volume 1 (1893) carried the subtitle *Bulletin of the Department of Geology*, a caption that persisted into the 1950s, although by that time this series was much more widely shared. Also on the masthead of the first volume appeared the designation of Andrew C. Lawson as editor, a responsibility that he shared in 1910 with John C. Merriam. When that distinguished paleontologist left the University in 1920 to head the Carnegie Institution of Washington, G. D. Louderback took the other half of the editorial chair and then carried on alone until he was joined by R. W. Chaney and H. Williams in 1931. UCLA did not gain editorial access until the mid 1950s, when Los Angeles editors were added; by 1960 a Los Angeles board was operating parallel to the Berkeley one. A University-wide Editorial Board was created in 1973 and presumably functions today. Issues, now down to two or three annually, reached volume 134 in 1989.

The fact that descriptive geology and paleobiology were originally situated in the same department resulted in a fairly balanced representation of these fields in the series for several decades. Lawson and Louderback published into the 1930s; Williams authored a series of vulcanological studies into the 1970s. But the prolific findings emanating from the Museum of Paleontology by Merriam and his associates and successors, among them E. L. Furlong, Chester Stock, B. L. Clark, W. D. Matthew, R. A. Stirton, Joseph T. Gregory, Samuel P. Welles, Donald E. Savage, Robert M. Kleinpell, and William A. Clemens, Jr., achieved a virtual monopoly, especially in more recent times. The first paper to constitute a single volume was the 322-page *Mio-Pleiocene Floras from West-Central Nevada* by D. I. Axelrod who, from Los Angeles, Davis, and Berkeley, has perhaps made the most consistently effective use of this series (1956–87).

Not only was a substantial portion of the geological features of western North America described and illustrated in this series, but also a significant part of the faunal and floristic discoveries made in the John Day Basin of Oregon and the Rancho La Brea asphalt beds of southern California.

Botany　This series commenced in 1902–3 with *A Botanical Survey of San Jacinto Mountain*, a master's thesis by H. M. Hall, who served on the Berkeley faculty for seventeen years before joining the Carnegie Institution of Washington. The first volume consisted principally, however, of a major paper by W. A. Setchell and N. L. Gardner on the algae of northwestern America—the first of their many pioneering studies of Pacific seaweeds. Setchell served as sole editor for the first two decades and then chaired an editorial board until his retirement in 1934. Essentially all departmental faculty and many graduate students were contributors during that period. If Setchell and Gardner's marine algae dominated for the first decade (continuing until 1937), this topic was superseded by T. Harper Goodspeed's contributions to the cytology of tobacco (*Nicotiana*) from 1912 to 1954. G. F. Papenfuss and his students picked up the algal theme in the mid 1940s and carried it forward to the 1970s. However, Herbert L. Mason, Adriance S. Foster, and Lincoln Constance and particularly their students and associates, were the most frequent authors in the 1940s, 1950s, and 1960s.

By all means the weightiest contribution was that of E. B. Babcock, with a two-volume, 1,030-page taxonomic treatment of the genus *Crepis*. This served as the basic document for the "school" of investigation of the genetics and evolutionary history of *Crepis* that flourished for many years. Perhaps the handsomest issue was that on the Mexican *Tigridia* by the late Elwood Molseed, a number of whose photographs of flowers were reproduced in color through a subscription campaign among his friends and colleagues. Volume 20 was exclusively a UCLA issue, which includes the classic Harlan Lewis and Margaret E. Lewis monograph of *Clarkia*. The Lewises' study was a fundamental element in the wide-ranging investigation of evolution in *Clarkia*, of which offshoots still appear in current journals. By the early 1960s, each contribution averaged at least 40 pages and was given a volume of its own.

The series, which consists of seventy-eight volumes to 1984, dealt primarily with the systematics, morphology, anatomy, cytology, ecology, and phytogeography of marine algae, ferns, and seed plants. Contributors included faculty, graduate students, and herbarium and garden staff members from at least five campuses.

Zoology   The history of the Zoology Series closely parallels that of the Botany Series. The first volume (1902–7) began with a paper by H. B. Torrey, *The Hydroids of the Pacific Coast of North America*, and contained articles by both W. E. Ritter and C. A. Kofoid, described as "from the San Diego Marine Biological Laboratory of the University of California." Ritter served as sole editor for the first four volumes and was then joined by Kofoid. Although Ritter moved permanently to La Jolla in 1909 as director of the newly founded Scripps Institution, he retained his editorial role for another decade and contributions from the marine laboratory are prominent in the series for many years. Studies of marine animals of the Pacific corresponded to the exploration of marine algae at the same period. The

Bulletin of the Scripps Institution of Oceanography, started in 1927 as a spin-off, continues.

Establishment of the Museum of Vertebrate Zoology in 1908 is reflected by the prompt appearance of the name of Joseph Grinnell, its director, as author of *The Biota of the San Bernardino Mountains*. From then on, the series alternated chiefly between publications on protozoan parasites by Kofoid, H. Kirby, and their students, and systematic and ecological studies emanating from the museum on various classes of vertebrates. A number of the early MVZ contributions dealt with the fruits of expeditions to Alaska and elsewhere sponsored by Annie M. Alexander. Volumes 14 and 23 recorded the findings of the 1912–13 Biological Survey of San Francisco Bay by the *Albatross*. T. I. Storer filled volume 27 (1925) with *A Synopsis of the Amphibia of California* in 342 pages. Occasional volumes were devoted wholly to contributions from UCLA.

This extensive series, which had attained volume 119 by 1988, has represented a broad range of zoological interests, both terrestrial and marine. Its emphasis has been on the systematics and behavior of organisms from foraminifera to fish, monkeys to tule elk, and birds and lemmings to lizards. Professors and graduate students alike from several campuses have found—and apparently still find—it a viable avenue for publication.

Entomology   The Entomology Series began in 1906 under the editorship of C. W. Woodworth and E. C. Van Dyke as a collection of technical papers from the Agricultural Experiment Station, dealing chiefly with insects of economic importance to the State of California. By the mid and late 1930s, however, there began to appear numerous largely taxonomic papers by E. G. Linsley and R. L. Usinger, soon to be joined by P. D. Hurd, J. W. MacSwain, and R. F. Smith. Usinger became one of the editors of this series in 1947 and retained that position almost until the time of his death in 1968; he also played a major role on the Editorial Committee itself. Linsley served as an editor during the 1950s and 1960s and contributed numerous papers, perhaps most notable the four-volume revision of the cerambycid (long-horn) beetles of North America, which totaled 490 pages with 158 figures.

The vast number and overwhelming diversity of insect groups represents a classical instance of the kind of data the series mode of publication handles best. Thesis-length, well-illustrated descriptive papers are a natural product of systematic entomological research. So great has been the demand for taxonomic investigations of insects that the *Bulletin of the California Insect Survey* was initiated to publish additional information on insects.

Despite the strong taxonomic emphasis of many of the papers, in recent years there has been increasing emphasis on biology, ecology, behavior, bionomics, hybridization, and evolution. The series on the comparative behavior of bees and the evening primroses in the southern California deserts by Linsley, MacSwain, P. H. Raven, and R. W. Thorp were a notable contribution to reproductive biology and co-evolution.

The entomologists seem to have been singularly successful in achieving early and maintaining subsequently a strong statewide proprietary interest in their series. Whether editorial supervision was in the form of north-south boards, statewide panels of advisory editors, or most recently an integrated all-University board, it worked effectively and harmoniously. It may be that the governing factor was the mutual need for a publication outlet of this character. The activity of the series shows a steep peak in the 1960s (forty volumes), a gradual decline in the 1970s (to twenty-five volumes), to a total in the 1980s of twenty-three volumes. Progress of a kind was attained with the introduction of "cladistic analysis" in volume 106 in 1986.

Ibero-Americana The distinguished series publication Ibero-Americana, founded in 1932 "to form a collection of studies in Latin American cultures, native and translated," is the epitome of multi-disciplinary effort. The original editorial board consisted of H. E. Bolton, A. L. Kroeber, and C. O. Sauer. Sauer, however, was its chief mover and remained on the board until his retirement twenty-five years later. The roster of editors over the years included Professors Lawrence Kinnaird, Arturo Torres-Rioseco, George P. Hammond, John Rowe, Lesley B. Simpson, Woodrow Borah, Sherburne Cook, James King, Luis Monguió, and James Parsons. In 1965, the editorial board was abolished in favor of a statewide panel, as in the other series.

The fifty-four studies published in the series dealt largely with Mexican ethnology, archaeology, demography, and historical and cultural geography. A particularly noteworthy contribution was the work of S. F. Cook, professor of physiology, who turned his remarkable talents as biologist, demographer, anthropologist, historian, and writer to the study of Indian populations and the massive changes brought about by European conquest. He found encouragement and assistance from Sauer, Simpson, Kroeber, and Robert F. Heizer in his demographic studies coauthored principally with Borah, who carried on their work into the 1970s. An editor of the *Hispanic American Historical Review* remarked in 1975, "The professions' debt to the authors for their work of the past three decades is incalculable" (HAHR 55:542).

Frugé commented that "a series of this kind, interdisciplinary but with a decided character of its own, can flourish only if it does belong to a close-knit group of people who have similar ideas about their research." This series was closely affiliated with the Center for Latin American Studies and involved many of the same personnel.

ADDITIONAL SERIES

In addition to the series in national history and anthropology, there were active series, both in the early days and later, in historical and humanistic studies of various kinds. Only two of these have survived, one in changed form. Linguistics, initiated in 1942, however, is still active.

Classical Studies   Since most of the early presidents of the University were professors of Greek or Latin, it is not surprising that publication began early in ancient history and literature. Among the very first in this category were the impressive if short-lived series in Graeco-Roman Archaeology (1902) and Egyptian Archaeology (1905), designed primarily to publish the results of expeditions financed by Phoebe Apperson Hearst, who also underwrote part of the publication cost. Large quarto, mostly cloth-bound volumes printed abroad, these probably would have been thought of as books if the president at that time had not been Wheeler.

An independent series, Classical Philology (1904) was created for shorter papers in literature and history. Authors involved, in addition to Wheeler himself, included such noted scholars as J. T. Allen, Monroe Deutsch, Ivan Linforth, and George Calhoun, who later became manager of the University Press. Yet another separate but less active series, Classical Archaeology, was set up in 1929. These two series were combined into Classical Studies (with new numbering) in 1965. The first volume was Part 1 of W. K. Pritchett's probably incomplete *Studies in Ancient Greek Topography*, a work that now comprises six parts with 1,337 pages of text and 858 plates. A special quality of these volumes, as well as of the same author's ongoing book series, *The Greek State at War* (4 vols., 1971–85) is Pritchett's defense of the ancient sources, particularly Herodotus, against modern critics. The late great historian, M. I. Finley of Cambridge, called Pritchett's work a "monument of erudition."

The thirty-three volumes of Classical Studies, together with the papers and monographs in the older series, add up to a huge amount of scholarly work in the classical field. Of related interest is an annual volume first edited by Pritchett himself in 1968 and entitled *California Studies in Classical Antiquity*. After the publication of twelve volumes, the annual in 1982 was converted into a journal, *Classical Antiquity*.

Perhaps most significant of all is the great book series Sather Classical Lectures, begun in 1921 and now consisting of more than fifty volumes.

Modern Philology   If patronage and persistence are convincing evidence that a particular series has found a useful role, Modern Philology, which was initiated in 1909 and had in 1989 attained volume 124, is surely a case in point. It is the last of several series to retain the term *philology* in its title. As a principal scholarly outlet for modern language departments, it has carried essays on literature, grammar, drama, riddles, and folklore in English, German, Spanish, French, Italian, and other languages. Some papers are thought to be more historical or descriptive than critical. Quite a number are edited texts of minor literary works. Nevertheless, it has enjoyed the active support of such worthies as R. Schevill, B. P. Kurtz, S. G. Morley, C. R. Bell, A. G. Brodeur, R. N. Walpole, and L. Monguió. Volume 11 (1922) was devoted to the Charles Mills

Gayley Anniversary Papers, commemorating Gayley's thirtieth year of distinguished service to the University.

This series has frequently precipitated editorial concern and debate. Although it is generally recognized that this outlet is useful to the language departments and has published distinctly first-rate monographs, there is widespread suspicion that there remains a residue of "reasonably competent works on topics of little interest." It is consequently suggested that, far from contributing to the growing distinction of the Press, such material may have tarred it with a reputation for publishing less than first-rate books and acting the role of that nemesis of all university presses, a house organ. Since many of the contributions are in languages other than English, it has also been proposed that it might be preferable to subsidize special printing by European firms, who are accustomed to doing such things.

However, no clear consensus has yet emerged and, in lieu of a better solution, the series continues to perform its historical function.

History   Although the History Series (1911–73) has not survived, it contained some notable works particularly in earlier years and ran to some eighty-three volumes. A precursor was the Publications of the Academy of Pacific Coast History (Bancroft Library), which issued four volumes between 1909 and 1919. The History Series itself comprised mostly volume-length studies, leavened by some shorter papers. Initial contributions often reflected departmental emphases on the history of the Spanish colonial period and the development and political organization of western America. Later they expanded to encompass events under the Roman Empire, eighteenth-century England, and a host of other times and places. Volume 19 (1929) was L. B. Simpson's notable *Encomienda in New Spain*, which was later reissued as a book and is still in print in paperback. Admired works on western American history included Adele Ogden's *The California Sea Otter Trade* (vol. 26, 1941); J. H. Kemble's *The Panama Route* (vol. 29, 1943); and R. H. Fisher's *The Russian Fur Trade* (vol. 31, 1943). All of these volumes were issued in cloth as well as in the paper covers traditional for series publication.

Perhaps no other series better illustrates the fate of the series form of publication, which appears to win and retain acceptance in some fields, not in others. In the late 1940s and 1950s, the Press expanded its book program to take advantage of the rapidly growing market for scholarly books. It now became possible to publish many of the stronger manuscripts as hard-cover books, leaving to the series those of lesser-known authors, which quickly became predominantly but not exclusively theses. However, the damage to the series was done, and it was eventually concluded that works in history should either succeed as books or not be published at all. Since then, the Press has greatly expanded its book publishing in American, English, European, and Asian history, and to a smaller extent in California history.

Linguistics Another area in the humanities where demand has remained strong, quality high, and serial monograph publication apparently broadly accepted is linguistics. The great majority of papers were products of the Survey of California Indian Languages, under the direction of Murray B. Emeneau and Mary R. Haas. They consist principally of dictionaries, grammars, and texts of Native American languages, often running to several hundred pages, with exotic or heavily accented typography, and often accompanied by tables and diagrams. It is noteworthy that it was Linguistics that pioneered in requiring camera-ready manuscripts and demonstrated that this can be a satisfactory method for publishing fully acceptable products in other series as well.

In the late 1960s, African languages and some contributions from South and East Asia began to be received, with a sprinkling of Slavic and Romance linguistics. The series forms an invaluable outlet for linguists, anthropologists, and some linguistically minded members of foreign-language departments, whose colleagues may very well publish under the rubric of Modern Philology. The use of this series has not only been maintained but has spread to at least six of the University's nine campuses and stands at 118 volumes currently.

One of the most recent contributions in this field is J. A. Matisoff's *Dictionary of Lahu*, a hill-dwelling Tibeto-Burman people, which runs to 1,576 pages, supplementing his 673-page *Grammar of Lahu*, making this among the best-documented minority languages of the world.

It seems clear that in Linguistics, as in the descriptive areas of natural history, the series form of publication provides a hospitable medium for handling large quantities of factual data. No one appears to have devised a superior method of handling material of this kind.

From time to time but particularly in the 1940s, there was pressure to establish an increasing number of new series, doubtless on grounds of equity. Why should only a few departments enjoy such a beneficent publishing service, whereas publication was a major concern of all faculty? Among the innovations were Child Development, Culture and Society, East Asiatic Philology, Folklore Studies (changed to Folklore and Mythology Studies in 1974 and continuing under that label), Industrial Relations, Linguistics, Mathematics (New Series), Microbiology, Music, Political Science, and Statistics. Not to be overlooked were the Agnes E. and Constantine E. A. Foerster Lectures on the Immortality of the Soul, which produced only three numbers in its very mortal single decade. English Studies (not to be confused with an older English series begun in 1929), Librarianship, and Sociology and Social Institutions were added in the 1950s. Occasional Papers, created in the 1960s, was designed as a catch-all to accommodate praiseworthy manuscripts for which an appropriate series was unavailable. The impracticality of trying to devise an editorial board for such a miscellaneous hodgepodge led to its discontinuance in 1976. Near Eastern Studies, established in 1963, remains active. Finally, the series entitled Catalogs and Bibliographies, established in 1981, is evidently responding to a real need.

DECLINE OF THE SERIES

Despite their long and distinguished history in the University, there is no question that the use and the importance of series publication have declined in the last several decades. A number of those founded during or even before the Wheeler era lost their attractiveness to authors and fell into relative disuse. Eventually they were recommended for termination by their sponsoring units or by the Editorial Committee itself as a consequence of one of its periodic reviews. Thus, Economics was discontinued after fifteen volumes, Education after eleven, History after eighty-three, Philosophy after twenty-four, Physiology after eight, Psychology after seven, and Semitic Philology after fourteen. Of the series established in the 1940s and 1950s, only Linguistics—currently at volume 118—found a useful niche and persisted; the others faded into disuse after issuing a single or only a few volumes.

In view of their history, why has use of the series declined so spectacularly? Was it suicide, mercy-killing, or merely progressive abandonment of a type of publication that is no longer necessary or relevant? There doubtless are innumerable answers, none of them complete or wholly satisfying.

The primary cause of decline was a change in emphasis in many of the natural sciences away from the synoptical, descriptive, and taxonomic aspects of the field, where the series had proven so successful. There is a general if inaccurate public perception that this aspect of investigation is "done," that the last geological formation has been mapped, the last "new" plant, bird, mammal, or insect discovered, the last Indian wrung dry of information. The tremendous stress on "reductionism" in both biology and the earth sciences in the past half century shifted attention away from diversity and detail, castigating it as "mere description." To be "modern," biology had to be molecular and cater either to biomedicine or to biotechnology; field geology lost out to geophysics and geochemistry. The current "reorganization" of biology at Berkeley that resulted in the termination of the century-old departments of Botany and Zoology, among others, is an extreme example (Pfaff 1989). The number of faculty members appointed in the areas adversely affected has declined proportionately as have the students; it is not always clear which came first. Not surprisingly, the series type of monograph has tended to retreat to the natural history museums, where its role continues to be important.

A second factor of major importance is the change in organization of the University from a single campus with well-defined, tightly knit departments to a more diffuse and multi-campus institution. Responsibility for a particular series became progressively diluted. University-wide committees, parallel committees, or panels were incapable of inspiring the pride of sponsorship of an earlier day.

Monographic publication appears to be more acceptable in some fields than in others. Particularly in the humanities and most social sciences, when the Press found it increasingly possible to offer the alternative of book publication to the better major manuscripts, series publication could not compete in prestige. Deprived of the better manuscripts, the series were sometimes left with what appeared to be lesser offerings, particularly student theses. When University Microfilms in Ann Arbor offered to make all dissertations available on film or by Xerox, the principal reason for publishing all but the very best student theses was greatly weakened. The consensus grew that, if a longer work could not make it as a book, it probably was not worth publishing at all, and the University imprint could only lose in luster if associated with such a product. The Editorial Committee had long ago decreed that the series should be reserved primarily for longer manuscripts, since shorter ones were suitable for journal publication. The vast increase in scholarly journals, both those sponsored by the Press and extramural ones, was in most areas of knowledge now sufficient to accommodate shorter articles. Thus, the series lost major manuscripts to book publication and shorter ones to journals of one sort of another.

An additional and more subtle factor was a change in the sociology of research. The series flourished on the sustained activity of highly individualistic investigators making deliberate progress in relatively long-term enquiries. Current emphasis, furthered both by extramural sources of funding and internal policies, is on "team research" and LPQs—the least publishable quantity—which commonly results in multi-authored progress reports of often-transient importance. These are judged to be "at the cut-

ting edge" of science and have to be published immediately, before they are overshadowed by their clones. Need-
less to say, series publication is an inappropriate vehicle for
them.

CURRENT STATUS

The transformation of the University Press from a service
agency designed to publish the work of the local faculty to
an actively competing academic publishing house has been
profound. Beginning under Samuel Farquhar and greatly
accelerating under the direction of August Frugé, who succeeded Farquhar in 1949, the Press has become a half century later a semi-independent scholarly publishing house,
certainly both one of the largest and one of the best. The
whole-hearted enthusiasm and effort of the editorial staff
and the Editorial Committee have long been concentrated
on continually improving and expanding a distinguished
book-publishing program.

Nevertheless, the Press has continued to publish what
remains of the old series monograph program. In all fields
where monographic publication retains prestige, the series
have survived and continue to do what the authors and research programs ask of them. All series now publish only
whole numbers, each designated a separate volume, so all
papers are of monographic length. Authors are asked to
provide camera-ready copy, which mitigates any charge
of overediting—some might prefer *more* copyediting—or
unnecessary delay. The distinction between series and

"separate works" has broken down almost completely. Paper-bound series have spawned hardback series, annual volumes, and journals. Insistence on camera-ready copy has made these various forms of presentation essentially interchangeable. Most important, no worthy manuscripts are being denied publication. The author is in a position to choose the most appropriate means for the publication of the fruits of his scholarship. Total series output in the last decade has averaged ten to twenty volumes annually, so their production remains a significant component of the Press's program.

At present the official list of series publications is as follows:

University of California Publications in
Anthropology
Botany
Entomology
Geography
Geological Sciences
Linguistics
Modern Philology
Zoology

University of California Publications:
Anthropological Records
Catalogs and Bibliographies

Classical Studies

Folklore and Mythology Studies

Near Eastern Studies

and

Bulletin of the California Insect Survey

Bulletin of the Scripps Institution of Oceanography

The Press now has a department of periodicals and serials, with an assistant director in charge. The Editorial Committee itself no longer looks at series manuscripts when they are submitted. The Press staff obtains reviews and forwards them together with the manuscripts to the individual boards, which make the decision to accept or reject. However, the Editorial Committee does have to vote the liens, and so retains the option of final oversight. Although the special series subcommittee, established in 1976, has not been reappointed in recent years, the principle remains, and this mechanism can be invoked whenever necessary.

Thus, in recent years the only distinction separating the series from other publications of the Press comes down to mode of distribution. What has happened to the "print-and-exchange" program of the Wheeler era? What has become of the incremental gain to the library's holdings that was deemed so essential in earlier years? The series volumes remain the backbone of the library's exchange program with some 4,220 institutions world wide, representing 250 countries. This is believed to be the largest exchange program of any university in this country, involving 16,680 titles. As always, exchange is most important with countries that lack a highly developed commercial book trade, where it is not only difficult to obtain publications but even to learn what has been published. By purchasing Press-issued series and journals at 10–20 percent of list price and imaginatively substituting other campus publications where necessary, the Berkeley Gifts and Exchange Division has succeeded in expanding its exchange program to the benefit of the entire University. Additionally, the authors have obtained global distribution of their writings, and the Press has not only recovered costs but also gained important items for its current lists.

The editorial subcommittee of 1975–76 concluded, "In our view, the University Press does have an obligation to publish the results of University scholarship. . . . We think a healthy program of Series publications should continue to be one of the available alternatives."

Happily, it still is. It remains to be determined what use will be made of the opportunity it provides.

REFERENCES

Frugé, A.
    1976. The service agency and the publishing house. Scholarly Publishing 7(2): 121–27.
    1986. The metamorphoses of the University of California Press, 24 pp. The Associates of the University of California Press, Berkeley and Los Angeles.

Muto, A. H.
  1976. The University of California Press 1893–1933, 175 pp.
        Ph.D. dissertation in Librarianship, Berkeley.
Pfaff, T.
  1989. California Q & A—a conversation with Beth Burnside.
        California Monthly 100(1): 8–10.
Report of the Subcommittee on Series Publication.
  1976. R. Berger, B. Berlin, H. Daly, D. Heiney, R. Kellogg,
        T. L. McFarland (ex officio), L. Constance (chair).
        23 April.

ANNOUNCEMENT

OF THE

UNIVERSITY OF CALIFORNIA PUBLICATIONS

BERKELEY
The University Press
October, 1904

I N the following list it is desired to make announcement of the various publications of the University of California, issued from the University Press. These publications com‐ prise a quarterly journal, some special works, and a number of scientific series. The latter appear at irregular intervals (making, however, uniform volumes) and contain the results of special research and investigation, chiefly by members of the University faculty.

In order to circulate these publications as widely as possible, thereby fulfilling their purpose as a medium for making public the results of scientific investigation, and also for the reciprocal advantage of the University Library, the Committee wishes to arrange exchanges with other uni‐ versities or scientific societies issuing publications in similar lines. To this end correspondance is invited and specimen copies will be sent on request.

The publications are also offered for sale as separate numbers or as complete volumes. The prices given include carriage. A copy of form for subscription or exchange is to be found on page 15 of this circular.

ANTHROPOLOGY.

The following series dealing with archaeological and ethnological subjects, are published under the direction of the Department of Anthropology, and embody the results of the explorations of the several scientific expeditions maintained by Mrs. Phoebe A. Hearst.

Graeco–Roman Archaeology.

Vol. I. The Tebtunis Papyri, Part 1. Edited by Bernard P. Grenfell, Arthur S. Hunt, and J. Gilbart Smyly. Pages 690, plates 9, 1903. . . Price, $16.00
Vol. II. The Tebtunis Papyri, Part 2. (In preparation.)

Egyptian Archaeology.

Vol. I. The Hearst Medical Papyrus. Edited by G. A.
Reisner and A. M. Lythgoe. (In press.)

American Archaeology and Ethnology.

Vol. I. No. 1. Life and Culture of the Hupa, by Pliny
Earle Goddard. Pages 88, plates 30   Price, $ 1.25

No. 2. Hupa Texts, by Pliny Earle Goddard. Price,   3.00

Vol. II. No. 1. The Exploration of the Potter Creek Cave,
by William J. Sinclair. Pages 27, plates 14,
.   .   .   .   Price,   .40

No. 2. The Languages of the Coast of California,
South of San Francisco, by A. L. Kroeber.
Pages 72   .   .   .   .   .   Price,   .60

No. 3. Types of Indian Culture in California, by
A. L. Kroeber. Pages 22   .   .   Price,   .25

No. 4. Basket Designs of the Indians of Northwestern California, by A. L. Kroeber. (In
press.)

Vol. III. The Morphology of the Hupa Language, by
Pliny Earle Goddard. (In press.)

Anthropological Memoirs. (Quarto.)

Vol. I. Explorations in Peru, by Max Uhle (in preparation.)

No. 1. Ruins of Moche.

No. 2. Huamachuco, Chincha, Ica, Pisco,
Huaitara.

No. 3. The Inca Buildings of the Valley of Pisco.

Special Volume.

The Book of the Life of the Ancient Mexicans, containing
an account of their rites and superstitions ; an
anonymous Hispano-American manuscript
preserved in the Biblioteca Nazionale Centrale, Florence, Italy. Reproduced in facsimile, with introduction, translation, and
commentary, by Zelia Nuttall. Part I, consisting of Introduction and Colored Fac-simile
of 80 pages. Part II, Translation and Commentary. (In press)   .   .   .   Price,   25.00

BOTANY.

The University of California Publications in Botany are edited by Professor William A. Setchell, and comprise for the most part botanical studies of California and the Pacific Coast. The price per volume is $3.50.

VOLUME I.

No. 1. A Botanical Survey of San Jacinto Mountain, by Harvey Monroe Hall. Pages 140, plates 14 Price, $ 1.00

No. 2. Two New Ascomycetous Fungi Parasitic on Marine Algae, by Minnie Reed. Pages 24, plates 2 Price .25

No. 3. Algae of Northwestern America, by W. A. Setchell and N. L. Gardner. Pages 253, plates 11 Price, 2.25

This is an exhaustive catalogue of the Algae of the Pacific Coast of Alaska and British America.

VOLUME II.

(In progress.)

No. 1. A Review of Californian Polemoniaceae, by Jessie Milliken. Pages 71, plates 11 . . Price, .75

No. 2. Contributions to Cytological Technique, by W. J. V. Osterhout. Pages 18 . . . . Price, .25

CLASSICAL PHILOLOGY.

There has just been started a series in Classical Philology edited by Prof. E. B. Clapp, Prof. W. A. Merrill and Dr. H. C. Nutting. The price per volume is $2.50 (about 300 pages). The first number just issued is:

VOLUME I.

No. 1. The Hiatus in Greek Melic Poetry, by Edward Bull Clapp. Pages 34 . . . . . Price, $ .50

EDUCATION.

The University of California Publications in Education, edited by Prof. Elmer E. Brown, deal with educational topics practical and theoretical.

VOLUME I.

Nos. 1-3. Notes on the Development of a Child, by Milicent
W. Shinn   .   .   .   .   .   .   Price, $ 2.25
A volume of 423 pages of special value to those interested in Child Study.

VOLUME II.

(In progress.)

No.   1. Notes on Children's Drawings, by Elmer E. Brown.
.   .   .   .   Price,   .50

VOLUME III.

(In progress.)

No.   1. Origin of American State Universities, by Elmer E.
Brown   .   .   .   .   Price,   .50

No.   2. State Aid to Secondary Schools, by David Rhys
Jones   .   .   .   .   Price,   .75
This monograph offers an account, drawn from original sources, of the history of State aid to academies, high schools, and other institutions of secondary grade, from the colonial period down to the year 1903, together with an account of the systems of extending such aid at the present time, in all the States which have taken advanced ground in this matter. The information which it contains will be found useful in the making of plans for the extension and improvement of State systems of secondary education.

GEOLOGY.

This series consists of papers containing the results of
investigations in the departments of Geology, Mineralogy
and Palaeontology, and is edited by Professor A. C. Lawson.
Price per volume, $3.50.

VOLUME I.

8   University of California Publications.

PATHOLOGY.

The pathological series of the University of California is edited by Professor A. E. Taylor and contains the results of investigations in the Hearst Pathological Laboratory, Affiliated Colleges, San Francisco.   Price per volume, $2.00.

VOLUME I.

No. 1. On the Quantitative Separation of the Globulins of Hemolytic Serum, with Special Reference to the Carbon Dioxide Group, by Clarence Quinan.

No. 2. Hydrolysis of Protamine with Especial Reference to the Action of Trypsin, by Alonzo Englebert Taylor.

No. 3. On the Synthesis of Fat Through the Reversed Action of a Fat-Splitting Enzyme, by Alonzo Taylor.   } In one cover.

No. 4. On the Occurrence of Amido-Acids in Degenerated Tissues, by Alonzo Englebert Taylor.

No. 5. On the Autolysis of Protein, by Alonzo E. Taylor.   } In one cover.

No. 6. On the Reversion of Tryptic Digestion, by Alonzo E. Taylor.

No. 7. Studies on an Ash-Free Diet, by Alonzo Englebert Taylor.

PHYSIOLOGY.

This series, edited by Professor Jacques Loeb, contains the results of investigations carried on in the Rudolph Spreckels Physiological Laboratory of the University of California.   Price per volume, $2.00.

VOLUME I.

No. 1. On a Method by which the Eggs of a Sea-urchin (*Strongylocentrotus purpuratus*) can be Fertilized with the Sperm of a Starfish (*Asterias ochracea*), by Jacques Loeb.

No. 2. On the Mechanism of the Action of Saline Purgatives, and the Counteraction of their Effect by Calcium, by John Bruce MacCallum.

No. 18. The Action of Cascara Sagrada (a preliminary communication), by John Bruce MacCallum.

No. 19. Artificial Parthenogenesis and Regular Segmentation in an Annelid (Ophelia), by G. Bullot.

No. 20. On the Action of Saline Purgatives in Rabbits and the Counteraction of their Effect by Calcium, (second communication), by John Bruce Mac-Callum.

No. 21. On the Local Application of Solutions of Saline Purgatives to the Peritoneal Surfaces of the Intestine, by John Bruce MacCallum.

In one cover.

No. 22. On the Toxicity of Distilled Water for the Fresh-Water Gammarus. Suppression of this Toxicity by the Addition of Small Quantities of Sodium Chloride, by G. Bullot.

ZOOLOGY.

The members of the Department of Zoölogy of the University of California embody the results of their investigations in a series edited by Professor W. E. Ritter. The University of California Marine Laboratory is located at San Diego where work is carried on both summer and winter. The price of the series is $3.50 per volume.

No. 1. The Hydroida of the Pacific Coast of North America, by Harry B. Torrey   .   .   .   .   Price, $ 1.00

No. 2. A Case of Physiological Polarization in the Ascidian Heart, by Frank W. Bancroft and C. O. Esterly
Price,   .10

No. 3. Embryology and Embryonic Fission in the Genus Crisia, by Alice Robertson   .   .   .   Price,   .50

No. 4. Correlated Protective Devices in Some California Salamanders, by Marion E. Hubbard.   .   Price,   .20

No. 5. Studies on the Ecology, Morphology, and Speciology of the Young of some Enteropneusta of Western North America, by Wm. E. Ritter and B. M. Davis
Price,   .50

No. 6. Regeneration and Non-Sexual Reproduction in Sagartia Davisi, by Harry Beal Torrey and Janet Ruth Mery   .   .   .   .   .   .   Price,   .15

No. 7. The Structure and Regeneration of the Poison Glands of Plethodon, by C. O. Esterly   .   .   Price,   .50

No. 8. The Distribution of the Sense Organs in Microscolex Elegans, by John F. Bovard.   (In press.)

ASTRONOMY.

Three series of publications, edited by Director W. W. Campbell of the Lick Observatory, include the results of investigations made by the Astronomical Department of the University, as follows :

Publications of the Lick Observatory.—Quarto.—Volumes I–VI completed. Volumes VII, VIII, and IX (in progress). Price, $3.00 per volume, post-paid. Volumes I and III are out of print.
Contributions from the Lick Observatory.—Octavo.—Volumes I–V all are out of print.
Lick Observatory Bulletins.—Quarto.—Volumes I and II completed; Volume III current, copies mailed as issued. Price, $2.50 per volume in advance. Volume I out of print.

AGRICULTURE.

The publications of the Department of Agriculture consists of Bulletins Nos. 1—— and Biennial Reports, edited by Professor E. W. Hilgard. These are sent gratis to citizens of the State of California. For detailed information regarding them address The Department of Agriculture.

UNIVERSITY CHRONICLE.

The University Chronicle is an official record of University life, issued four times during the year. It includes addresses delivered at Berkeley and elsewhere by members of the faculty and also prominent members from other institutions who are here temporarily. Six volumes have been completed. Price, per year, $1.00.

UNIVERSITY CALENDAR.

The University Calendar is the vehicle for making official University announcements, and contains also notices of special lectures, meetings of societies, athletic, musical, literary and other student activities. It is issued weekly throughout the college year. Price, per term, post-paid, 25 cents.

UNIVERSITY REGISTER.

The University Register, containing the admission requirements, courses of study, catalogues of faculties and students, regulations, and other information concerning every department of the University.   Price, 25 cents.

OTHER UNIVERSITY PUBLICATIONS.

Elementary Studies in Literature for adult classes, by Cornelius
      Beach Bradley   .   .   .   .   .   Price, $ .10

Annual Announcement of Courses of Instruction in the Aca-
      demic Colleges   .   .   .   .   .   Price,   .10

Annual Announcement of the Summer Session in the Academic
      Colleges.

Catalogue of Officers and Students in the Academic Colleges.
      Published in September and in February   Price,   .10

President's Biennial Report.

Secretary's Annual Report.

Index

Academy of Pacific Coast History (Bancroft Library), 38n3
Accounting, 89, 108, 111, 225–26
Acquisitions. *See* Manuscript selection and procurement
Administrative and academic publications, 49, 50, 62, 100, 104–5, 188, 194, 199
African studies, 237
After the Hunt, 222
AIGA Book Show. *See* Fifty Books of the Year Exhibition
Ainsworth, George J., 11, 35
Alexander, Annie M., 41, 253
Allen, Albert H., 31–32, 45, 48, 62n8, 63, 66, 67, 69, 78, 179; as copyeditor, 64–65; critical of Wheeler's monograph press, 82–83; first manager of the Press, 59–60; and publication exchange, 243–44
Alphabet, and Elements of Lettering, The, 152
American Archaeology and Ethnology (A. A. & E.) Series, 38, 40, 247, 249
American Chemical Journal, 8
American Historical Association, 140
American Institute of Graphic Arts (AIGA), 166–67. *See*

also Fifty Books of the Year Exhibition
American Journal of Mathematics, 8
American Journal of Philology, 8
Ancient Libraries, 152
Angell, James B., 5
Animal Life in the Yosemite, 42, 80
Anniversary publications, University of California. *See* Semicentennial Publications; Seventy-fifth anniversary publications
Anthropological Records, 248, 249
Anthropology, Department of, 39–40, 73; twentieth anniversary publication, 248
Anthropology, Museum of, 39–40, 78, 248
Anthropology series, 40, 247–49
Anza's California Expeditions, 86
Archaeological Excavations in Fiji, 248
Archibald, Katherine, 185
Arizona Flora, 221
Arnheim, Rudolf, 185–86
Art and art history, 177, 185–86, 221–22, 237
Art and Visual Perception, 185–86
Art of the Northwest Coast Indians, 221

Library of Congress Cataloging-in-Publication Data

Muto, Albert.
  The University of California Press : the early years, 1893–1953 /
Albert Muto.
    p. cm.
  Based on the author's dissertation (University of California,
Berkeley, 1976).
  "A Centennial book"—P.
  Includes bibliographical references and index.
  ISBN 0-520-07732-6 (alk. paper)
    1. University of California Press—History.   2. University
presses—California—Berkeley—History.   3. Scholarly publish-
ing—California—Berkeley—History.   I. Title.
Z473.U623M88   1992
070.5'94—dc20   92-20506
                                                            CIP

Designer: Barbara Jellow
Compositor: Wilsted & Taylor
Text: 11/16 Janson
Display: Janson
Printer: Edwards Brothers, Inc.
Binder: Edwards Brothers, Inc.